P9-DDV-857

Praise for *Fixing the Game*

"Roger Martin has written a book that is at once original, insightful, and inspirational. With his 'tell-it-as-it-is' bluntness, he chronicles the failures of modern day capitalism and offers clear and realistic policy recommendations for 'fixing the game' and building a better world for investors. If you enjoy wit and seek wisdom, this is the book for you."

—John C. Bogle
Founder and former chief of The Vanguard Group

"We've gone from an economy based on making things to one based on making things up, with Wall Street remodeled as a casino in which the expectations market, reflected in stock prices, has become more important than the real market in which real factories are built, real products are developed and sold, and real dollars show up on the bottom line. Roger Martin offers a riveting account of how the expectations game is beginning to destroy the real game, threatening the future of American capitalism. Through his brilliant analysis of the NFL (which will entrance even those who don't follow the market), he shows us how we can get back to the real game of building for the present and the future. *Fixing the Game* is a must-read for all who care about business being a positive agent for change in the world. And that should be all of us."

—Arianna Huffington
Co-founder and Editor-in-Chief, *The Huffington Post*

"*Fixing the Game* is an essential book, one that should be read by leaders in the business community and financial regulators worldwide. Martin identifies the insidious trap that can so easily seduce entrepreneurs and CEOs—the temptation to simply trade value rather than create it—and provides clear, compelling advice on how to keep focused on the real game—of creating and satisfying customers, running a business legally and ethically, and staying true to a well thought out 'real world' strategy."

—Nandan Nilekani
Chairman, Unique Identification Authority of India and
former CEO, Infosys Technologies Limited

"*Fixing the Game* artfully links theory and practice, and reminds us that getting both right is important if we are going to fix capitalism. Roger Martin asks provocative questions about what constitutes good management, and forces the reader to consider the ways in which elegant logic or a compelling theory actually undermines commonsense business practice. And along the way he identifies changes—in regulation, business, and governance— that will realign private incentives with the public good."

—Judith Samuelson
Executive Director, Business and Society
Program at the Aspen Institute

"*Fixing the Game* provocatively analyzes the fascinating intersection between seemingly disparate American institutions—the NFL and Wall Street. Martin brings together the worlds of finance and professional football in a richly compelling story of investors, game changers, and the best ways to fix broken markets. For football fans, business leaders, and policymakers alike, this cautionary tale shows how easy it is to game a sports contest or a market, and how the NFL's structure and policies started by legendary Commissioner Pete Rozelle can be the key to maximizing customer value and healing American capitalism."

—Paul Tagliabue
Commissioner of the NFL, 1989–2006

"At last, a gust of fresh air from one business school leader blowing away some of the intellectual smoke supporting compensation and market practices that have come to place American-style capitalism at risk. Roger Martin effectively punctures the illusion that executive stock options, speculative hedge funds, and the single-minded pursuit of stockholder value can build a strong, competitive economy."

—Paul Volcker
Former Chairman of the Federal Reserve

FIXING
THE GAME

ROGER L. MARTIN

FIXING
THE GAME

BUBBLES, CRASHES, AND WHAT CAPITALISM
CAN LEARN FROM THE NFL

Harvard Business Review Press

Boston, Massachusetts

No part of this publication may be reproduced, stored in or introduced into a retrieval system, or transmitted, in any form, or by any
means (electronic, mechanical, photocopying, recording, or otherwise), without the prior permission of the publisher. Requests for permission should be directed to permissions@hbsp.harvard.edu, or
mailed to Permissions, Harvard Business School Publishing,
60 Harvard Way, Boston, Massachusetts 02163.

Library of Congress Cataloging-in-Publication Data

Martin, Roger L.
Fixing the game : bubbles, crashes, and what capitalism can learn
from the NFL / Roger Martin.
    p. cm.
Includes bibliographical references.
ISBN 978-1-4221-7164-6 (alk. paper)
1. Corporations—United States.   2. Industrial management—
United States.   3. Corporate governance—United States.
4. Capitalism—United States.   5. Financial crises—United States.
6. National Football League—Management.   I. Title.
HD2785.M3577 2011
658.4—dc22   2010051658

The paper used in this publication meets the requirements of the
American National Standard for Permanence of Paper for Publica-
tions and Documents in Libraries and Archives Z39.48-1992.

To Jennifer Frances Martin . . . Always

CONTENTS

ONE

FIXING A BROKEN GAME

We would accomplish many more things if we did
not think of them as impossible.

—Vince Lombardi

When a financial bubble bursts, there's a run on scapegoats. With hundreds of billions of dollars in wealth
wiped away in short order, it's natural to look for someone
to blame. So, after each economy-shaking crash, the U.S.
Congress goes after the evildoers with determination and
vigor. In 1929, it targeted the brokers who fueled a speculative bubble with easy loans and abundant hype. In 2000,
the villains were unscrupulous dot-com CEOs, peddlers
of counterfeit value that never existed. And in 2008, it
was executives at big investment banks, who created
inscrutable derivatives from worthless mortgages.

In each case, Congress called the culprits to account at
a series of acrimonious hearings, the purpose of which

was to sniff out the reasons for the crash and to prevent a recurrence. Each time, once-cocky executives, now suitably humbled, faced the censure of Congress inside committee rooms and crushes of angry reporters outside them. In the aftermath, Congress worked to change regulations to ensure that future players could not engage in the kind of dangerously risky behavior that had led to each crash.

It happened after 1929, after 2000, and after 2008—and the aftershocks of the 2008 crash are still being felt. For a clearer view of the pattern, think back to the year 2002. The economy was reeling. The NASDAQ, which sat at 5,132 on March 10, 2000, had lost two-thirds of its value by the middle of 2001, and finally bottomed out at 1,114 in October 2002—80 percent off its high. The more stable and conservative Dow Jones Average, which had peaked at 11,723 on January 14, 2000, plummeted to 7,702 by July 2002.[1] Overall, the dot-com crash lopped an estimated $5 trillion of market capitalization from American companies.[2]

As the economy cratered and scores of new-economy companies declared bankruptcy, the search for scapegoats was on. It didn't take long to identify those charlatan senior executives and to vilify them en masse. But a few were singled out for particular blame: No one company symbolized the excesses of the dot-com era—and the disastrous effects of its end—like Enron. And so no executive faced the anger of Congress quite like Ken Lay.

A loquacious and charming character, Lay had been chairman of Enron Corporation for more than a decade and had become a central figure in its undoing. Under Lay's leadership, Enron had embraced all the opportunities of the much-hyped "paradigm shift" to the Internet era, transforming from a boring, old-economy energy company to a new-age, market-making, Web-enabled powerhouse. By 2000, Enron was racking up $101 billion in annual revenue and had a market capitalization of $66 billion. *Fortune* named it America's most innovative company six years running, and it was regularly selected as one of the country's best places to work.[3] But, by the end of 2001, it was all over. That December, Enron filed for Chapter 11 bankruptcy reorganization and was, for all intents and purposes, worth nothing.[4]

Billions of dollars of shareholder wealth had vanished. Thousands of laid-off employees held now worthless pensions. Yet Lay, his CEO Jeff Skilling, and his CFO Andrew Fastow had made away with hundreds of millions of dollars, thanks to stock options cashed in during the precrash heyday. How could it have happened? How had Enron's board of directors and auditor Arthur Andersen let things go so far wrong? Was it complicity or ineptitude? And, more important, was Enron an isolated case of criminals run amok, or was its failure reflective of much bigger issues? To answer these burning questions, Congress called a multitude of hearings to grill everyone involved.

So it was that on February 12, 2002, after numerous delays, Lay found himself sitting in the Senate Commerce Committee hearing room. Well aware of the mood of the country, the senators used their introductory remarks to rip into Lay, calling him "a confidence man" unworthy of the job of carnival barker. After ninety minutes, Lay was given the floor and promptly refused to answer any questions, invoking his Fifth Amendment rights against self-incrimination.[5] Subsequent testimony did little to calm public or congressional outrage, as members of the board and outside auditors claimed management had fooled them and even Enron whistle-blower Sherron Watkins testified that Lay was "a man of integrity" who had no idea what was going on in his own company.[6]

In the wake of the Enron hearings, the government determined that it needed to take bold and tough action to make sure that there would be no repeat of this kind of mess. The damning testimony suggested there were two particularly murky problems to be dealt with: oversight and executive compensation.

On the oversight front, Congress and regulators saw a raft of compromises and conflicts. In principle, a board of directors is elected by the shareholders to represent their interests and hold those running the company to account. Similarly, an auditor is retained to provide independent financial oversight. The Enron debacle had exposed serious cracks in this structure. Board members either didn't take their jobs seriously or were unhelpfully partial to management, allowing executives to enrich themselves to the detriment of the company. Auditors weren't sufficiently independent either; they made more money from consulting to the company than from auditing its financial statements, which meant that auditors too had very strong incentives to agree with management, even to the point of overlooking financial statement fraud.

Then there was the issue of executive compensation. Companies were increasingly providing incentives in the form of stock options, with the idea that managers would be motivated to perform well and improve the business, thereby increasing the value of their options. Because these options didn't need to be expensed by the company, they were essentially free to issue, making them a very attractive and widely used compensation alternative—especially in Silicon Valley, the epicenter of the tech bubble. But these options created a problem: they gave management a huge upside reward for improved company performance but no real downside punishment for weak performance. In other words, stock option rewards gave managers the incentive to take risky actions: if the risks worked out, the managers got rich; if they didn't, the managers were largely unaffected, regardless of the damage to the company. Even if the poor performance didn't reflect very well on their decisions, managers could always argue that trends outside of their control—irrational competitors, macroeconomic shifts, and so on—had caused the damage.

The consensus in Washington was that the dot-com crash was caused by lax and conflicted oversight and by problematic compensation schemes, both of which enabled those huckster CEOs to run amok. Given that diagnosis, a series of new regulations could be introduced to fix the problems.

To address the oversight issue, Congress passed the Sarbanes-Oxley Act on July 30, 2002. SOX, as it became known, had wide-reaching effects. It mandated greater independence of boards, particularly their audit committees. It forced companies and their auditors to engage in painstakingly thorough internal controls assessment and certification. It intimidated the auditing firms (except one) into divesting their consulting arms to rid themselves of inherent conflict. It required CEOs and CFOs of public companies to sign and take personal liability for the accuracy of their financial statements. Take that, Ken Lay!

Shortly after SOX became law, the Financial Accounting Standards Board (FASB) took aim at the rampant use of stock options as executive compensation. New rules mandated that stock option grants would now be expensed on company income statements, meaning they were no longer quite so "free." Meanwhile, compensation experts piled on, advocating a move from all-upside stock option incentives to *phantom stock* incentives (technically called *deferred share units* or *restricted share units*), which gave the recipient a cash amount equivalent to the price of the stock at a specified later time, typically at retirement. These instruments were seen to correct the problem with stock options, because the manager who received them would feel both the upside and downside, just like the investor. Finally, board governance experts began to encourage substantial stock ownership by independent board directors, so that the directors' interests would be more closely aligned with those of the shareholders. Companies promptly and wholeheartedly followed the advice of these experts, keen to avoid an Enron-like demise.

In the end, a whole series of regulatory changes were adopted to prevent a future crash. Scapegoats were trotted out before Congress, root causes were determined, and laws and corporate norms were changed to address those causes. The stock market crash of 2000–2002 had been the most precipitous since 1929, some seventy years before. With new regulations implemented to fix the oversight and compensation problems that had created the dot-com market bubble, the hope was that at least another seventy years would pass before another such disaster.

Sadly, it would be less than a decade. Not only that, the next stock market meltdown would be considerably worse than the 2000 version; the next crash would threaten to bring down the entire global financial system. This time, rather than a tech bubble, it was a mortgage bubble. This time, it wasn't just the erosion of a secondary market like NASDAQ; it was a meltdown in the broader index, with the S&P 500 down 40 percent in the second half of 2008 alone. This time, it didn't mark the disappearance of a bunch of new and relatively unknown firms like Freeinternet.com; rather, this time, venerable and prominent companies like Bear Stearns and Lehman Brothers were wiped away. In fact, some of the largest firms in the world, such as Citibank, AIG, and Bank of America, would have disappeared in 2008 if not for massive government bailouts. This time, the U.S. economy needed massive infusion of spending to recover, even as it led the world into a deep recession.

ASKING THE RIGHT QUESTION

In the wake of such a spectacular crash, less than a decade after the last, one might have expected that observers would ask, What did we do wrong the last time? Why didn't our fixes, put in place to prevent another devastating crash, do what they were intended to do? How, with all of those independent and motivated directors, empowered and unconflicted auditors, and massive control procedure certifications, did this mess manage to happen again? Why didn't the CEO sign-offs and beautifully aligned incentive compensation structures work to prevent undue risk-taking and malfeasance on the part of financial executives? Is it possible that our changes addressed symptoms, rather than root causes? One might have expected that we would ask these hard questions. Yet we really haven't.

We haven't looked deeper into blameworthy CEO behavior to understand what *really* caused it. We haven't examined the broader theories that underpin our economy and that informed all of those ineffective fixes after the last crash. Instead, we've looked for a new scapegoat, chosen to operate from the same fundamental theories, and doubled down on the same fixes. We've said, "Darn it; we didn't clamp down hard enough on these companies. They took risks they simply should not have taken. Clearly, they still have oversight problems and compensation problems. Regulations are too loose and it is time to clamp down even harder."

Consequently, following the 2008 crash, more new regulations and norms have been (and will be) introduced to improve oversight and manage executive compensation with the aim of preventing a future crash. And few of these efforts will help. In fact, coming down harder on the financial services sector by increasing capital adequacy ratios, imposing a clearer regulatory oversight structure, and so on won't decrease the chance of yet another market meltdown in any meaningful way. It's true that the next crash won't be caused by irrational exuberance over new-economy stocks or by the securitization of subprime mortgages; we've fixed those particular triggers for now. But as long as we fail to understand the real, fundamental reasons behind those crashes, and the bubbles that preceded them, it is only a matter of time until we will have the next crisis.

The only way we can avoid increasingly frequent stock market meltdowns—and all the pain, suffering, and economic dislocation they cause—is to explore the theories that underpin American capitalism. Our theories about the fundamental goal of corporations and the optimal structure of executive compensation are fatally flawed and have created stock market upheavals. Acting on these theories, we have built structures into our capital markets system that threaten the future of American capitalism.

THE ORIGINS OF OUR CURRENT THEORY

In 1976, finance professor Michael Jensen and Dean William Meckling of the Simon School of Business at the University of Rochester published a seemingly innocuous paper in the *Journal of Financial Economics* entitled "Theory of the Firm: Managerial Behavior, Agency Costs and Ownership Structure."[7] The authors likely had no idea that it would go on to be the single most frequently cited article in business academia and that it would form the prevailing theory of the role of the firm and proper compensation in our society today.

The article first defined the *principal-agent problem* and created *agency theory*. In the authors' construct, shareholders are the *principals* of the firm—i.e., they own it and benefit from its prosperity. Executives are *agents* who are hired by the principals to work on their behalf. The principal-agent problem occurs because the agents have an inherent incentive to optimize activities and resources for themselves rather than for their principals. For example, an executive might declare her own time to be so valuable that she requires a private jet to ferry her around. While this might be convenient for the executive, and may even increase her productivity level, it may well hurt the owners of the company, reducing earnings by more than the increase in productivity. Such a choice puts an agent's interests ahead of those of the principals and creates an *agency cost*.

Jensen and Meckling argued that when executives squander firm resources to feather their own nests, the result is both bad for shareholders and wasteful for the economy. Instead, the theory goes, the singular goal of a company should be to maximize the return to shareholders. To achieve that goal, the company must give executives a compelling reason to place shareholder value maximization ahead of their own nest-feathering. While it is not possible to entirely eliminate the self-interest of executives, the authors posited that we could better align that self-interest with the interests of shareholders; we could eliminate agency costs by giving agents meaningful amounts of stock-based compensation, actually making them shareholders as well as executives. Executives would then be *very* interested in increasing shareholder value, because when it increased, so would their own compensation.

Like all good theories, agency theory had limitations and unexpected side effects, a fact its disciples have chosen to ignore (though Jensen himself has acknowledged them).[8] In particular, the theory had the unfortunate effect of tightly tying together two markets: the real market and the expectations market.

The *real market* is the world in which factories are built, products are designed and produced, real products and services are bought and sold, revenues are earned, expenses are paid, and real dollars of profit show up on the bottom line. That is the world that executives control—at least to some extent.

The *expectations market* is the world in which shares in companies are traded between investors—in other words, the stock market. In this market, investors assess the real market activities of a company today and, on the basis of that assessment, form expectations as to how the company is likely to perform in the future. The consensus view of all investors and potential investors as to expectations of future performance shapes the stock price of the company.[9]

Historically, professional managers played entirely within a single market: they were in charge of performance in the real market and were paid for performance in that real market. That is, they were in charge of earning real profits for their company and they were typically paid a base salary and bonus for meeting real market performance targets.

Compensation rooted in the expectations market used to be rare. In 1970, for example, stock-based incentives accounted for less than 1 percent of CEO remuneration.[10] But that all changed after the advent of agency theory. Implicitly, Jensen and Meckling had argued that the way to spur executives to best perform their duties in the real market was to make their pay significantly dependent on the performance of the company in the expectations market. This was a critical shift. After 1976, executive compensation became increasingly stock based, so that when executives produced a stock price increase in the expectations market, their compensation rose dramatically. In 2009, for instance the highest-paid CEO in American was Larry Ellison of Oracle, and estimates suggest that 97 percent of his paycheck came from realized gains on options.[11] Ray Irani, CEO of Occidental Petroleum, earned $31 million in 2009, including $1.17 million in base salary, a bonus of $1.2 million, and restricted stock awards of just under $25 million.[12] It has become an accepted premise of good governance that, in order to properly align their incentives with those of the shareholders, executives and board members must receive a substantial portion of their pay in the form of stock-based compensation. The crashes of 2000–2002 and 2008–2009 did nothing to diminish this premise; in fact, they strengthened it.

A SMARTER GAME WITH A BETTER THEORY

Few people conceive of the world of business in terms of real and expectations markets. Yet, there is another world in which the distinction between a real market and an expectations market is much more profoundly understood—the National Football League (NFL). While it isn't a perfect metaphor for business, it is a highly instructive one.

The NFL is, far and away, the most successful sports league in America. Regular season NFL games regularly garner higher ratings than the final round of golf's Masters, the Kentucky Derby, the Daytona 500, baseball's all-star game, the most watched National Basketball

Association final game, and college basketball's Final Four title game.[13] The 2010 Super Bowl was the most-watched television event in history, with more than 106 million American viewers.[14] According to *Forbes*, of the twenty-five sports teams worth more than $1 billion, nineteen are from the NFL. No sport comes close to the NFL's economic power.[15]

In the NFL, the real market operates when teams take to the field on Sunday and play a game for sixty minutes, making real runs, passes, blocks, and tackles. Real touchdowns and real field goals are scored. There is a real winner and a real loser. Coaches and players are in full control of what happens in the real game (referees notwithstanding).

Then there is the NFL's associated expectations market: gambling. Gamblers try to guess who will win a given game on a given Sunday and place bets based on that expectation. If the game were to be played between two equally matched opponents, we would expect that roughly half of the bettors would select one team to win and half would select the other—creating a perfectly efficient market with a balance of bets on each side.

Of course, that rarely happens. One team is playing on the road, one team has a stronger quarterback or has a poor rush defense. So the Las Vegas bookmakers—the folks who run the expectations market—dynamically balance the bets on either side through the use of a *point spread*. If more people expect that the Dallas Cowboys will beat the Detroit Lions, the bookies will give points to the Lions. This means, if you're betting, that instead of betting on Detroit to win the game, you bet that Detroit will either win the game or, importantly, lose by less than the point spread. Imagine that the point spread is Dallas by 4.5 points. If you wager on Dallas to win, Dallas would need to win by 5 or more points for the bet to pay off. If you bet on Detroit, the Lions would need to win or lose by 4 or fewer points for the bet to pay off. From the time betting opens until kick-off, the point spread moves according to the bets placed, settling to a point of equilibrium where roughly half the money is bet on Detroit and half on Dallas.

The point spread in football is the analog to a stock price in business. The collective expectations of all participants in the market determine both a point spread and a stock price. If more bettors put money on the favored team, the point spread will increase; if more investors buy a stock at a given price, the stock price will rise. In both the NFL and in business, as the real game grew in stature and prominence, the expectations game became more and more sophisticated. In both cases, dedicated individuals emerged to ply their trade in the expectations market, becoming NFL bookies or bettors, capital markets brokers or investors.

But unlike American capitalism, the NFL looked thoughtfully at the relationship between the real game and the expectations game and identified a serious danger. After the 1962 season, Paul Hornung, the Green Bay Packers halfback and the league's most valuable player (MVP), and Alex Karras, a star defensive tackle for the Detroit Lions, were accused of betting on NFL games, including games in which they played. Pete Rozelle, just a few years into his thirty-year tenure as league commissioner, responded swiftly. He suspended Hornung and Karras for a full season, and fined five Lions players who admitted to placing $50 bets on that year's Championship game between the Packers and the Giants.[16] Rozelle also created NFL Security—what is often called the NFL's FBI—to work with law enforcement agencies across the country to detect and stamp out player involvement in betting on the NFL.

Why did Commissioner Rozelle take such a definitive stand against players and coaches betting on football? He must have envisioned the consequences if he didn't. Let's imagine that the Lions are playing against the Minnesota Vikings, and the Lions are favored to win by 10 points. The Lions players know their team is better than the Vikings and will almost certainly win the game. So, one of them conspires with some unscrupulous bettors to wager millions of dollars on the Vikings. The player then does all he can to ensure that the Lions win the game, but by 9 or fewer points. He has engaged in the art of *point shaving*, sacrificing a few points of advantage in order to win the game by a lower margin than the prevailing point spread. And he's made a lot of money for his friends.

Executed with precision, point shaving doesn't damage the team's record in the real game. But imagine if the culprit *is* willing to hurt his team's record in the real market for a short period; in that case, he could try to cause his team to lose a couple of straight games— a practice colorfully known as *tanking*—so that the subsequent point spread is relatively easy to beat. He could then bet on winning that subsequent game and make a killing.

By altering the on-field dynamics, point shaving and tanking have the potential to undermine the integrity of the league and dramatically diminish the experience for fans. Rozelle recognized this, and so did all he could to prevent them from taking root in his league.

Rozelle and the team owners observed that even though the expectations game of betting on football sprang from the real game, it was played by very different rules. They clearly saw that the pressures of the expectations game could do serious damage to the real game. Like a parasite that eventually kills its host, sports betting had the ability to destroy the sport. So Rozelle and his successors, Paul Tagliabue and Roger Goodell, have enforced a strict separation between the real market and the expectations market; everyone involved in the real game of football—players, coaches, and officials alike—are forbidden to have anything to do with betting on football—on their own games or on other teams' games. Even spending time with known gamblers and bookies is strongly discouraged.

In other words, the NFL has managed the division between the real and expectations market in a manner that is exactly the opposite of the way we have managed it in business. American capitalism encourages, and in many cases even mandates, the players in the real game to invest heavily in the expectations game, and has built structures that bring the key players from the two markets into almost constant contact. CEOs are given significant (if not overwhelming) amounts of stock-based compensation to ensure that they focus first and foremost on shareholder value maximization. Those same CEOs interact with capital-market participants frequently, providing guidance to them about likely future performance so that folks can place their bets—oops, that's make their trades—with appropriate information.

Imagine an NFL coach holding a press conference on Wednesday to announce that he predicts a win by 9 points on Sunday, and that bettors should recognize that the current spread of 6 points is too low. Or picture the team's quarterback standing up in the postgame press conference and apologizing for having only won by 3 points when the final betting spread was 9 points in his team's favor. While it's laughable to imagine coaches or quarterbacks doing so, CEOs are expected to do both of these things. In fact if they don't, the CEO and company can be slapped on the wrist by regulators and even sued for not alerting shareholders that their expectations for the quarter were off the mark. In American capitalism, a tight connection between the real and expectations markets is now ensconced in our legal framework.

Of course, one could argue that the games of football and business are sufficiently different, that CEOs can't engage in activities like point shaving and tanking after placing bets. Or can they? With respect to point shaving, it is clear that CEOs and CFOs do steer their companies to the consensus earnings forecast of the Wall Street analysts. If shareholder value is what matters, then they will deliver exactly what is expected of them in that arena, real performance be damned. Consider the following trend: in the 1980s, CEOs met corporate guidance about 50 percent of the time; by the mid-1990s, they did so 70 percent of the time.[17] Companies are getting better and better at meeting expectations exactly. And rarely do companies surpass expectations by a significant measure. Why? Because if a company beats expectations this quarter, the expectations will be that much higher for the next quarter and that much harder to meet. The capitalist incentive for point shaving is at least as strong as it would be in the NFL, and there is good reason to believe that plenty of CEOs do it, and often.

Tanking happens in companies too. CEOs rarely miss their consensus forecast by a small margin. They either hit the "number" or they fall short by a long shot. In effect, they tank; they take a big fall in one quarter in order to reset expectations at a much lower level, which allows them to perform wonderfully against that low base of expectations.

THE PROBLEM WITH EXPECTATIONS

Point shaving and tanking in the capital markets are genuine issues, but they pale in comparison with an even greater problem. Recall that modern capitalism dictates that the job of executive leadership is to maximize shareholder value, as measured by the market value of the company's stock. To that end, the CEO should always be working to increase the stock price, to raise expectations about the company's prospects ad infinitum. And just how does that play out?

To see, let's return briefly to football. In 2007, the New England Patriots had a remarkable year; the team went unbeaten in the regular season, racking up a stellar 16-0 record. Eight of its starters went to the Pro Bowl. Quarterback Tom Brady was named the league's most valuable player, and head coach Bill Belichick earned coach of the year honors. Brady threw more touchdown passes than had ever been thrown in a season, and receiver Randy Moss set the record for most touchdown catches in a year. The team scored more points that season than any team in history. It was, in short, a superlative performance. In terms of the real market, the Patriots were perfect.[18]

But the Patriots' performance in the expectations game was mediocre in comparison. In betting vernacular, a favored team *covers the spread* when it wins the game by more than the point spread. In their sixteen-win regular season, the Patriots covered the point spread only ten times. Why? Because expectations ran away to unattainable levels. The Patriots had started the season with sensible expectations and played, admittedly, exceptionally well. The average point spread for the first eight weeks was 10.5, and the Patriots were able to cover the spread in every game, winning by an average of 20.5 points. But as they continued to perform very well, expectations rose; bettors expected the Patriots to continue to be more and more exceptional each week. The point spreads widened, and before long the Patriots were facing the largest spreads in the history of the NFL.

They played very well in the second half of the season, though less exceptionally than in the first half of the season. They still won each game, but in the final eight weeks, the Patriots beat opponents by a comfortable but somewhat lower 12.5 points on average, while point spreads had risen to an average of 16.5. Against these heightened expectations, the Patriots covered the point spread in only two of their eight games in the second half of the season. Brady's Patriots thrashed the Dolphins 28-7 in the second-to-last game of the season, but still couldn't meet bettors' expectations for a win by 22 points or more.[19]

The lesson is that no matter how good you are, you cannot beat expectations forever. Expectations will get ahead of anything you can actually accomplish, even with superhuman effort. Patriots quarterback Tom Brady had perhaps the finest season of any quarterback in NFL history, but he couldn't beat expectations more than ten of sixteen times. And that is why quarterbacks aren't compensated on the basis of how they perform against the point spread. While Tom Brady was leading his team to a perfect record but only beating expectations ten times out of sixteen, his young counterpart on the Cleveland Browns, Derek Anderson, was leading his team to a decent but unspectacular 10-6 record on the field, but a superb 12-4 record against the spread.[20] If the point spread mattered more than the real game, Anderson, whose team missed the playoffs, would have out-earned Brady, who took his team to the Super Bowl championship game and set records doing so.

The problem is, in American capitalism, CEOs *are* compensated directly and explicitly on how they perform against the point spread; that is, against expectations. Imagine the following scenario: a company decides to pay its CEO $10 million in total compensation for the year. It could pay that CEO $10 million in salary or, alternatively, it could pay him $2 million in salary and $8 million worth of phantom stock units (say 100,000 units with the stock at $80 per share). The simple $10 million salary embodies no incentive to increase shareholder value, while the $2 million salary plus phantom stock embodies a large incentive to do so. If the CEO can double the price of the stock by the time he retires, he will have earned $18 million in that year rather than $10 million.

Recall that the company's stock price is $80 per share today because expectations of the company's future performance have coalesced there. Any existing shareholder who had a more doubtful view of future expectations would sell the stock, cease to be a shareholder, and in the process drive the stock price lower. If anyone had a more optimistic view of future expectations, that person would offer to buy the stock at more than $80 per share and drive the price up. The CEO's phantom stock units are valued at

$80 per share because, in aggregate, current expectations suggest that is exactly what the stock is worth.

The CEO now has a clear and simple incentive: to raise expectations of future performance from the current level. There is no other way to increase the value of his incentive compensation. One might imagine that improving performance in the real market would increase the stock price, but this just isn't the case. The dot-com bubble taught us that stock price and real market performance are not as closely linked as we would like to believe. Even setting that fact aside, consider that investors already tend to believe that a company will improve its performance in the real market over time and therefore build that belief into the stock price. And if investors already believe that real performance will improve over time, actually improving real performance doesn't *exceed* their expectations, it merely *meets* them. Sadly, improving real performance doesn't help much in creating shareholder value.

Microsoft provides a good illustration of this conundrum. Over the past decade, Microsoft has performed quite spectacularly in the real market. It has nearly tripled its revenue and profit (see figure 1-1). However, with a few brief exceptions, Microsoft stock (adjusted properly for splits) has traded in a narrow range between $20 and $30 a share for the entire decade of spectacular real-market performance.[21] The market expects Microsoft to perform pretty much spectacularly in the real market, and so doesn't reward it in the stock price for doing so (see figure 1-2).

FIGURE 1-1

Microsoft revenue 2000–2010

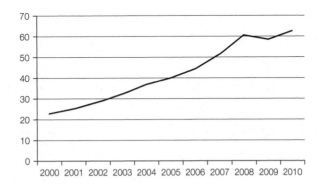

Source: Microsoft earnings releases.

FIGURE 1-2

Microsoft share price, 2000–2010

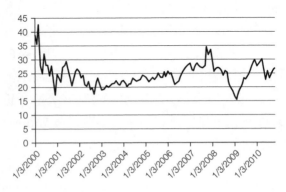

Source: Yahoo! Finance.

EXECUTIVE BEHAVIOR

The proponents of shareholder value maximization and stock-based executive compensation must have imagined that these theories would focus executives on improving the real performance of their companies and thus increasing shareholder value over time. Yet, these goals have prompted nothing of the sort. Let's assume that an executive is indeed motivated by realizing a good return on her stock-based incentive compensation (because if she's not, it was a waste to offer it in the first place). What would lead her to do the hard, long-term work of substantially improving real-market performance when she can choose to work on simply raising expectations instead? Even if she has a performance bonus tied to real-market metrics, the size of that bonus now typically pales in comparison with the size of her stock-based incentives. Expectations are where the money is.

And of course, improving real-market performance is the hardest and slowest way to increase expectations from the existing level. The company has to build facilities, hire employees, invest in advertising, and wait for these all to convert to real sales and profits increases—at a level above what is already expected by the stock market.

There are much easier ways to increase expectations. The easiest is to hype your stock on Wall Street by providing aggressively high guidance on the company's projected earnings. Just slightly harder is switching to a more aggressive accounting treatment to make the company's real performance look better than it is. Some such changes are simply aggressive, others are illegal. And indeed, since 1976, the incidence of large-scale accounting fraud by public companies has increased dramatically. Why? Because executives have millions of reasons to do whatever they can to increase expectations of future earnings.

But even with the twin tools of earning guidance and accounting rule changes, executives can't keep expectations on the rise forever, nor can they continue to meet them as they grow forever. Like Tom Brady in 2007, CEOs may well see market expectations radically outpace what can be achieved by even the best management team. Look at Cisco Systems and its star CEO John Chambers. Chambers spent the first decade of the twenty-first century consistently building share and increasing profits. And how did the stock price react to this real-market performance? It fell from a high over $80 per share in March 2000 to just $20 per share at the end of 2010, destroying hundreds of billions of dollars of shareholder value. Expectations for Cisco in the year 2000, when it set the record for the highest market capitalization in history (over $550 billion), were simply unachievable, no matter how well Cisco went on to perform.[22]

Those expectations were fueled by an exuberance utterly outside Cisco's control.

In the face of expectations that can run wild, CEOs have increasingly focused on what they can control: managing share price over the short run. Shareholders, on the other hand, should want CEOs to focus on the long term, on increasing share price more or less forever. So it turns out that rather than aligning the interests of shareholders and executives, stock-based compensation has reinforced the agency problem it was created to solve. What's more, it has destroyed long-term shareholder value by driving shorter and shorter horizons of decision making, and even contributing to shorter CEO tenure. CEOs know that expectations are likely to fall, so they have incentive to leave or retire in order to cash in stock-based compensation instruments while expectations are high.

Even the best of CEOs can fall prey to the expectations game. Indisputably, one of the most successful CEOs of the last century was Jack Welch, who ran General Electric (GE) from 1981 to 2001. Welch became a poster boy for shareholder value maximization when he gave a profoundly influential speech on the subject at New York's Pierre Hotel shortly after his appointment as CEO. Though he didn't use the term *shareholder value* explicitly, the speech marked a clear shift to a profits-first focus. Welch went on to transform GE from a slow-growth firm with a market capitalization of $13 billion into the most valuable company in the world, worth $484 billion at his retirement, when he left with an estimated $900 million worth of GE stock from his incentive compensation.[23]

Welch grew his company and made it more profitable—good, tough real-market stuff. But he also retired at the very peak of his company's stock price, after a short-term run-up in value. GE has never come close to approaching the market capitalization it had at Welch's retirement. In fact, despite almost a decade of hard work by his successor Jeff Immelt, GE's market capitalization is still not half the level it was when Welch left.

SO WHAT?

Focusing executives on shareholder value maximization using stock-based compensation was supposed to give shareholders a better deal. The theory ran that shareholders' returns were diminished by agents and the agency costs they impose. So we imposed a whole new set of rules to mitigate those agency costs and increase the return to shareholders. Yet, it simply hasn't worked out that way. Total returns on the S&P 500 for the period from the end of the Great Depression (1933) to the end of 1976, the beginning of the shareholder-value era, were 7.5 percent (compound annual). From 1977 to the end of 2010, they were 6.5 percent—suggesting that shareholders have little to celebrate, despite having been made the clear priority.[24]

But it isn't just about the money for shareholders, or even the dubious CEO behavior that our theories encourage. It's much bigger than that. Our theories of shareholder value maximization and stock-based compensation have the ability to destroy our economy and rot out the core of American capitalism. These theories underpin the regulatory fixes instituted after each market bubble and crash. Because the fixes begin from the wrong premise, they will be ineffectual; until we change the theories, future crashes are inevitable. New theories that recognize the important distinction between the real market and the expectations market, and that return our focus to the real market, are needed.

The difference in outcomes between a real-market focused world and an expectations-market dominated world is stark and critically important for the economy. When the real market is dominant, customers are the focus and the central task of companies is to find ever better ways of serving them. Entrepreneurs who create customer value through innovations in products, services, and business models, like Thomas Edison or Henry Ford, earn the highest rewards. When the expectations market is dominant, traders are the focus and gaming markets is the task; regardless of what happens, traders make money. In our current, expectations-oriented world, market makers or specialists are consistently among the most profitable businesses in America, earning supernormal returns year after year, even when the markets plummet and the rest of us lose. For instance, hedge fund managers James Simons and John Paulson each made over $2 billion in personal compensation in 2008 while markets were plummeting.[25]

The real market produces a positive-sum game for society. Everyone can be better off as more and more value is created for customers. In contrast, the expectations market produces a gigantic zero-sum game. In trading, by definition, for every dollar won, there is a dollar lost. It therefore pits players against one another to split up a defined, finite pie. In the expectations market, the goal is to make a trade in which you have an upper hand, regardless of the impact on the other party.

In the real market, there is opportunity to build for the long run rather than to exploit short-term opportunities, so the real market has a chance to produce sustainability. Because the real market is grounded in real people, real companies, real employees, real factories, and so on, it shifts slowly without huge volatile swings. A great year in the real market is 4 percent economic growth, and a bad year—like 2008—is 3 percent shrinkage. But because expectations have no bounds, the expectations market swings wildly with huge volatility.

While the economy shrank modestly in 2008, stock prices dropped 50 percent.

The real market produces meaning and motivation for organizations. The organization can create bonds with customers, imagine great plans, and bring them to fruition. The expectations market, on the other hand, generates little meaning. It is all about gaining advantage over a trading partner or putting two trading partners together, then tolling them for the service. This structure breeds a kind of amorality in which information is withheld or manipulated and trading partners are treated as vehicles from which to extract money in the short run, at whatever the cost to the relationship. And over time, in trading businesses, since there isn't opportunity to build something positive for the world, the motivation migrates to earning as much compensation as possible.

The real market contributes to a sense of authenticity for individuals. Because individuals can find meaning in their jobs, in that they can build value for customers while benefiting shareholders and generating sustainability, they can feel that they are living authentic lives. They can be open about their motives and plans, because they are not playing a zero-sum game but are doing something real and positive for society. They can create meaning, for themselves and others. The expectations market generates inauthenticity in its participants, filling their world with encouragements to suspend moral judgment. Executives are asked to dedicate themselves to doing that which they cannot do—that is, to keep expectations rising forever. They receive incentive compensation to which the rational response is to game the system. And since they spend most of their time trading value around rather than building it, they lose perspective on how to contribute to society through their work. Customers become marks to be exploited, employees become disposable cogs, and relationships become only a means to the end of winning a zero-sum game.

In short, a real-market orientation creates individual and societal good, while an expectations orientation creates a downward spiral that threatens both individual well-being and the health of our economy. American capitalism is in danger, and the danger stems directly from the way we have linked the real world to the expectations world, amplifying the influence of the expectations market on the real market.

By tying together the real and expectations markets, we have created an environment in which many companies focus more on their stock analysts than on their customers. In this environment, executives are pressured to live inauthentic business lives, pandering to a stock market that they know they cannot please for long, even as they cut jobs and expenses to make this quarter's consensus earning numbers. It is a world in which employees feel ever less loyalty to their company, knowing that their company has precious little loyalty toward them. As employees see their peers laid off in the busts and new folks hired in the boom, they become acutely aware that it is the transaction that matters and the money behind it, rather than the relationship.

As the lives of corporate leaders grow ever more inauthentic, more and more of our executives begin to disregard their moral compass entirely and engage in scandalous, illegal behavior. The accounting scams of 2001–2002 as practiced by Enron, WorldCom, Tyco International, Global Crossing, and Adelphia amounted to the biggest business scandal in at least a generation. But rather than marking the beginning of a period of calm in which executives learned from the crisis and reset their moral compasses, the scandal served as a warning sign of what was to come. Only a couple of years later, the options backdating scandal erupted, in which hundreds of companies and executives engaged in utterly reprehensible and illegal activity related to compensation schemes. And only few years after that, the economy was engulfed by the subprime mortgage crisis, in which numerous firms immorally and illegally skirted regulations and turned a blind eye to the consequences of those actions.

In addition to bad behavior by real-market players, our short-term, expectations focus also produces intense volatility in the expectations market. Following seventy years of relative stock market stability, we have had two extreme meltdowns in less than a decade. And all of that upheaval has created an opportunity for a new kind of market player, one that exists solely to exploit current volatility and to produce yet greater levels of it. These are the hedge funds, which make billions in profits from volatility, taking advantage of less-sophisticated investors while creating no net value for society.[26]

Overall, a pervasive emphasis on the expectations market has reduced shareholder value, created misplaced and ill-advised incentives, generated inauthenticity in our executives, and introduced parasitic market players. The moral authority of business diminishes with each passing year, as customers, employees, and average citizens grow increasingly appalled by the behavior of business and the abundant greed of its leaders. At the same time, the period between market meltdowns is shrinking, and regular investors are growing ever more skittish. Meanwhile, more capital and more talent are flowing into hedge funds, which continue to exploit and even cause volatility in individual stocks and broader indices. It is a pretty sorry picture and one that has little chance of getting better with the current theories in place.

The capital markets—and the whole of the American capitalist system—hang in the balance. The expectations game is beginning to destroy the real game, slowly from within. But it isn't too late. American capitalism can get back to the real game, back to funding and building companies to create meaningful products and services that customers care about. It can switch its attention from the zero-sum expectations market to the positive-sum real market.

FIXING THE GAME: FIVE POSITIVE STEPS

There are five major things we need to do to heal American capitalism, to fix the game and get real again:

1. We must shift the focus of companies back to the customer and away from shareholder value. In other words, we must turn our attention back to the real market and away from the expectations market. This shift necessitates a fundamental change in our prevailing theory of the firm. The current theory holds that the singular goal of the corporation should be shareholder value maximization. Instead, companies should place customers at the center of the firm and focus on delighting them, while earning an acceptable return for shareholders.

   Our current capital markets regulatory approach focuses on shareholders, not customers, and stresses the importance of letting free market forces prevail, even if some of those forces threaten to destroy the market. On this front, we can take an important page from the NFL playbook. The NFL manages and regulates the league with a focus on the fans, putting a product on the field that is maximally enjoyable and stimulating for its customers. And it understands that the game must be tweaked continuously to keep ahead of those who would seek to game it. We would do well to emulate the NFL's approach here. This shift in mind-set and regulatory approach will be pursued in chapter 2.

2. We must restore authenticity to the lives of our executives. A focus on customers rather than shareholders will be a move in the right direction—it creates meaning and deep intrinsic motivations. But in addition to shifting our theory of the firm, we must rethink our models of executive compensation. Stock-based compensation creates a powerful incentive to do something that executives have come to understand is undoable—keep expectations rising continuously. The result is that executives are pushed toward managing expectations more so than real performance. To do so effectively, they end up leading inauthentic lives and doing work

devoid of deeper meaning, which is bad for their companies and themselves. We must eliminate stock-based incentive compensation and create new models that focus executives on real and meaningful goals, goals that enable those executive to live and work in a balanced, authentic manner. This challenge will be the subject of chapter 3.

3. We need to address board governance. Boards of directors profoundly influence the performance of a company and its executives, and we need to recognize that current theory concerning boards of directors is fundamentally flawed. These days, we treat the board as a vehicle to overcome the principal-agent problem. In fact, in the wake of the 2000–2002 crash, Congress invested boards with much more responsibility for ensuring that executives are managing for the benefit of share-holders. But even a cursory examination shows that, like executive management, boards are composed of agents. And if executives are agents, creating agency costs, how does the employment of another group of agents—called the board of directors—discipline the first group of agents and reduce agency costs? There is no good answer to the question, which means it is time to

fundamentally rethink the role and structure of boards. Transforming board governance will be the subject of chapter 4.

4. We need to regulate and manage expectations market players more effectively, most notably hedge funds. Net, hedge funds create no value for society. They have huge incentives to promote volatility in the expectations market, which is dangerous for us but lucrative for them. So, we need to rein in the power of hedge funds to damage real markets. We need to better regulate the relationships between hedge funds and pension funds, and ensure that our huge pension funds don't create incentive structures for hedge funds that damage pensioners. Regulating expectations market players, including hedge funds and pension funds, will be the subject of chapter 5.

5. Business executives need to take on a more expansive and positive view of the role of for-profit companies in society. The prevailing shareholder value maximization theory isn't terribly helpful; it creates a narrow view of the role of business and minimizes the contribution of business to society. A new framework, one that better enables executives to think about the greater role of business in society, is needed. In

chapter 6, such a framework will be introduced to provide a theory and a tool for management executives to contribute positively to society while serving their shareholders well.

American capitalism is at a critical juncture. Our leaders have embraced a persuasive but ultimately flawed theory to construct their understanding of the economy, the model of executive compensation and the role of business. This theory leads us inexorably down a path to greater volatility, less value creation, and minimal authenticity. But it is by no means impossible to turn things around. In 1976, the business world embraced a new theory of the firm that transformed the game. It can do so again. It can embrace a different conception of business. It can devise a new model for executive compensation. It can create new structures that support, rather than fight against, authenticity and meaning. It is a matter of devising a new theory of the firm, and shifting our focus and behavior toward that understanding. In doing so, we can fix the game.

TWO

MAXIMIZING CUSTOMER DELIGHT

There is only one valid definition of a business purpose: to create a customer.

—Peter Drucker, *The Practice of Management*

On April 20, 2010, the *Deepwater Horizon* oil well, under lease to BP, exploded in the Gulf of Mexico, killing eleven workers and spewing crude oil into the water. BP quickly went into damage-control mode, blaming the rig owners, Transocean, for safety lapses. BP then went on to attempt to minimize the scope of the damage, as CEO Tony Hayward explained: "The Gulf of Mexico is a very big ocean. The amount of volume of oil and dispersant we are putting into it is tiny in relation to the total water volume."[1] By the end of May, Hayward, clearly tired of being pilloried by the media and the U.S. government, finally apologized. Asked what he would say to the Gulf residents who had seen their livelihoods affected by the spill, Hayward responded: "The first thing to say is I'm sorry. We're sorry for the massive disruption it's caused their lives. There's no one who wants this over more than I do. I would like my life back."[2]

Unsurprisingly, the apology was overshadowed by Hayward's astonishing tin ear—complaining about his own hardships even as he attempted to acknowledge BP's regret to those in the Gulf region. It would take months to finally cap the blown-out well, by which time it had released the equivalent of almost 5 million barrels of oil into the Gulf. Not just a disaster for the environment, the *Deepwater* spill proved to be one for BP as well. It's become a case study of how not to handle a public relations crisis.

Thankfully, we have long had a case study of how we *should* handle even the most unimaginable crisis, courtesy of Johnson & Johnson (J&J). On September 29, 1982, a twelve-year-old girl in Chicago died after taking a capsule of J&J's Extra-Strength Tylenol. Six other deaths followed shortly thereafter, and police soon linked all seven deaths to Tylenol, hypothesizing that a single murderer had placed bottles of cyanide-laced Tylenol on the shelves of Chicago-area drug stores and supermarkets. It appeared that the tampering was limited to Chicago, but no one knew how many bottles were affected, who had done the tampering, or why it had happened.

J&J was in a terrible bind. Tylenol represented almost a fifth of the company's profits, and any decline in its market share would be difficult to reclaim, especially in the face of rampant fear and rumor. Yet, rather than attempt to downplay the crisis—it was after all, likely the work of an individual madman in one tiny part of the country—J&J did just the opposite. Chairman James Burke immediately ordered a halt to all Tylenol production and advertising, distributed warnings to hospitals across the country, and within a week of the first death, announced a nationwide recall of every single bottle of Tylenol on the market. J&J went on to develop tamper-proof packaging for its products; an innovation that would soon become the industry standard.

Burke's response is often touted as a show of great personal integrity, one that led the company to make the right, albeit profoundly difficult, choice in the face of terrible uncertainty. So the question is: how was Burke able to navigate through the worst crisis of his career and emerge unscathed—celebrated, even—while BP's Hayward was transitioned out of a battered, weakened company with his reputation in tatters? What led Burke to respond in one way and Hayward so dramatically in another? Was Burke simply a moral paragon, able to see what others could not and bravely act on his own conviction? Or, was something else at play?

It is too easy to say that Burke was a saint and Hayward was not. Rather, Burke and Hayward acted as they did because each was directed to do so by his company's abiding purpose. In the wake of the *Deepwater Horizon* spill, Hayward's actions suggest that BP's profits were at the heart of its crisis response plan. The company's values statement, as articulated on its public Web site, begins, "BP wants to be recognized as a great company— competitively successful and a force for progress." It goes on to describe BP as "progressive, responsible, innovative, and performance driven."[3] *Competitively successful* and *performance-driven* are typically code for shareholder value–oriented priorities, so it stands to reason that protecting the company's share price and financial viability was paramount. Hayward acted as he did because shareholder value theory told him to do so. All of his actions— limiting liability, distributing blame elsewhere, and attempting to minimize the scope of the problem—were an attempt to protect his shareholders. Yet, despite all of Hayward's efforts, BP lost more than half of its market capitalization between April and July of 2010.

At J&J, Burke's actions were also deeply informed by his company's vision, a vision he saw literally every time he walked through the lobby of his headquarters. There, engraved in granite, are the words of legendary J&J

chairman Robert Wood Johnson, articulated in 1943 in preparation for the company's initial public offering and enshrined as the company's credo ever since:

> *We believe our first responsibility is to the doctors, nurses and patients, to mothers and fathers and all others who use our products and services . . . We are responsible to our employees, the men and women who work with us throughout the world . . . We are responsible to the communities in which we live and work and to the world community as well . . . Our final responsibility is to our stockholders. When we operate according to these principles, the stockholders should realize a fair return.*

The pecking order is clear and unambiguous: customers come first, employees are second, communities third, and shareholders absolutely last.

Given the prevalence of shareholder value theory in our modern economy, J&J's credo is a shocking articulation of very different priorities. With those priorities in mind, Burke had no choice but to do all he could to protect J&J's customers—even if those actions might put profits at risk. He forged ahead with an unprecedented recall, long before all the facts were clear or careful planning could be done, knowing that the capital markets might see it as an extreme and costly overreaction. He proceeded, well aware that the recall might be an implied admission of guilt, putting the company in legal harm's way and exposing its shareholders to substantial losses. Yet Burke followed the credo regardless. Customers came first and stockholders came fourth—and he acted accordingly. He didn't put "meet quarterly profit expectations" at the top of his list. In fact, he put it squarely at the bottom. And how did his shareholders do in the end? Although sales of Tylenol took a huge hit in the months immediately after the recall, J&J's share price was largely unaffected by the crisis. And, as the new tamper-proof Tylenol packages hit the shelves, market share quickly rebounded.

As it happens, J&J's investors seem to do just fine, crisis or no. J&J is one of the fifteen most valuable companies in the world, as measured by market capitalization, meaning that it has created as much shareholder value as virtually any company in the world.[4] In fact, it created the tenth-highest value of any company that chose to set up shop in anything other than energy or banking.

The world tends to believe that shareholders will benefit only if they hold first place, at the very core of the business. Yet, that prevailing theory simply does not hold in the case of J&J. J&J not only puts shareholders last, it doesn't even talk about maximizing their value. It only states that they "should earn a fair return." Notice it isn't "*will* earn a *great* return," but "*should* earn a *fair* return."

Of course, one example isn't enough to prove that putting the shareholder behind the customer (and others) turns out to be good for shareholders. But J&J demonstrates that a company can be very explicit about putting customers first, yet still be able to create enormous value for shareholders. Interestingly, two more of the most valuable companies in the world are also quite explicit about putting shareholders behind customers, though they do so in a slightly less pointed manner than does J&J.

Procter & Gamble (P&G) declares in its purpose statement: "We will provide branded products and services of superior quality and value that improve the lives of the world's consumers, now and for generations to come. As a result, consumers will reward us with leadership sales, profit and value creation, allowing our people, our shareholders and the communities in which we live and work to prosper."[5] For P&G, consumers come first and shareholder value naturally follows. Per the statement of purpose, if P&G gets things right for consumers, shareholders will be rewarded as a result.

Then there's Apple. Its CEO, Steve Jobs, seems to delight in signaling to shareholders that they don't matter much and that they certainly won't interfere with Apple's pursuit of its original customer-focused purpose: "to make a contribution to the world by making tools for the mind that advance humankind."[6] Jobs's feisty, almost combative demeanor at shareholder meetings is legendary. At the meeting in February 2010, one shareholder asked Jobs, "What keeps you up at night?" Jobs quickly responded, "Shareholder meetings."[7]

Of course, Apple, P&G, and J&J are not paragons of virtue. All three companies have stumbled from time to time. Apple was investigated for backdating options.[8] P&G faced hundreds of lawsuits after the Rely tampon was linked to toxic shock syndrome.[9] In 2010, J&J was criticized for being slow to act in issuing a series of recalls related to product quality.[10] People are fallible, even when guided by meaningful statements of purpose. But when three of the fifteen most valuable companies in the world—companies that have clearly outpaced their peers on the creation of value for shareholders—are explicit about not seeking to maximize shareholder value, something interesting is happening.

THE MAXIMIZATION CHALLENGE

The purpose of a company, as articulated by shareholder value devotees, is shareholder value maximization. Yet Apple, P&G, and J&J all successfully focus on customers instead of shareholders. This suggests that there is a choice to be made: maximize return to shareholders or maximize some customer measure. But is it a choice? Couldn't a company focus on both? Couldn't a company place equal emphasis on shareholders and customers, making them both the top priority? Wouldn't that deliver even better returns?

It sounds wonderfully appealing, but such an approach is undone by the notion at the heart of shareholder value theory. It states that a company must *maximize* the value it creates for shareholders. A company can't make customers and shareholders equal top priorities in this construct, because it can only maximize one thing at a time. It is exceedingly difficult and maybe entirely impossible for a human being, organization, or even computer to maximize two separate and distinct outcomes at the same time.[11]

Think of an oil refinery that wants to maximize the dollar value of the products (such as unleaded gasoline, heating oil, and jet fuel) it produces from an incoming barrel of oil. The refinery would like to get the greatest revenue out of each barrel that it runs. Yet, there are constraints on what it can produce, including the mix of products its customers demand, the quality and quantity of crude supply, its own economic resources, its capacity, and so on. Given the constraints, determining the optimal mix requires a massive computational effort. And that's only for any one decision, not taking into account the hundreds of optimization decisions that need to be made in a large company every day. It's more complexity than our puny human brains can typically manage. So a mathematical technique called linear programming was developed to quickly and efficiently optimize a given output, subject to other constraints.

The very nature of constraints dictates that we can only maximize one thing at a time—for example, the total volume of the output, or the profitability of the output, but not both. Perhaps heating oil is the fastest and easiest output to produce. So, if we want to maximize volume, we produce only heating oil. But heating oil offers a lower profit margin than jet fuel, so if we care more about profits than volume, we would produce jet fuel instead. Heating oil produces the greatest volume, jet fuel the greatest profit; but we can't concurrently produce 100 percent heating oil and 100 percent jet fuel, so we can't maximize both profit and volume at the same time, no matter how sophisticated our linear program is. We have to pick one main objective function and treat the others as minimal constraints.

The only exception to this rule is when one of the variables is a subset of another. For example, if I ask you to take a 16-gram ball of clay and maximize both the number of 1-gram spheres and the number of 1-gram cubes you create with it, it will be impossible for you to do it. The more spheres, the fewer cubes; it is as simple as that. If instead I ask you to maximize the number of both objects and spheres, this you can do, because *sphere* is a subset of *object*. You can make sixteen spheres and in doing so also produce sixteen objects (see figure 2-1).

FIGURE 2-1

Clay object optimization

Optimization
Maximize the number
of spheres or cubes

Option 1

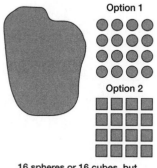

Option 2

Optimization with constraints
Maximize the number of spheres,
subject to the constraint of at
least 4 cubes

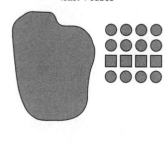

16 spheres or 16 cubes, but
not both

12 spheres and 4 cubes; the
maximum number of spheres
is constrained

Optimization with subsets
Maximize the number of
spheres and objects

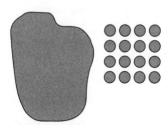

16 objects and 16 spheres; because
spheres are a subject of object, two
functions are maximized at once

THE PRIMARY OBJECTIVE OF BUSINESS

Just as a business must choose how to optimize its production resources, it must also choose its primary objective, its ultimate purpose. It has to choose between making shareholder value its primary goal, subject to meeting a basic customer value hurdle, and making customer value its main goal, subject to creating a minimally acceptable level of shareholder value.

Shareholder value theory is unambiguous in this regard: it states that a company's obligation is to put shareholder value maximization first. At a bare minimum, the company must deliver to its customers a rate of return on the market value of the equity (i.e., on the prevailing stock price) that is above the risk-adjusted cost of equity. In other words, if a stock is trading at $100 on January 1 and the risk-adjusted cost of equity is 15 percent, the company must increase the share price by $15 over the course of the year in order to have achieved its minimum acceptable return for shareholders. If the stock is worth less than $115 on December 31 (assuming no dividends were paid), observers (and those who compile total shareholder return statistics) will declare that the executive team hasn't increased shareholder value sufficiently.

This framework has even entered the regulatory environment, through U.S. rules governing financial reporting. In June 2001, the Financial Accounting and Standards Board (FASB) issued Statement 142, which changed the way auditors treat intangible assets (like intellectual property and trade secrets) and goodwill (like a company's reputation with its clients). Previously, companies had to write down intangible assets and goodwill over time on a fixed amortization schedule. FASB 142 ended this practice and mandated that auditors would instead have to declare annually whether intangible assets and goodwill were "impaired" or had retained their value. If they were impaired, the auditors would have to write the assets down to reflect current market value.

Given the new regulations, auditing firms have had to develop a procedure to determine whether an asset is or is not impaired. The most straightforward approach would be to stay grounded in the real market, making an estimate of the company's discounted future cash flows and comparing that with the net book value of the company's assets. If the discounted cash flows were lower than their book value, then a write-off would be necessary. However, perhaps lured by the siren song of shareholder value, auditing firms have mixed the expectations market into the equation. Auditors compare the discounted future cash flows with the current shareholder value—as determined by the current stock price. If they deem shareholder value to be too low relative to the estimated discounted cash flows, the auditors would have cause to mandate a write-down of the firm's assets to a level consistent with shareholder value.

As a consequence, CEOs who fail to manage upward the expectations of shareholders risk being forced to take a sizable write-down on their company's assets—the announcement of which could very well set off a downward spiral of yet lower expectations and further write-downs. So firms have clear incentives to place shareholder value front and center as the primary objective of the organization.

And, to be fair, the argument for shareholder value maximization has a clear logical elegance. Common shareholders take on risk by investing in the company. Everyone else gets paid first. By legal construct, the shareholders are residual claimants—they get paid only after all other claimants are satisfied. Thus, shareholders deserve to have the company work to maximize the value of their residual claim. It is as simple and elegant as that. And this logic is buttressed by the compensation model that flows out of agency theory. We use stock-based compensation to align the interests of executives with those of the shareholders so that the executives will actually seek to maximize shareholder value rather than to maximize their own rewards.

Interestingly, the shareholder value maximization argument is entirely theoretical rather than empirical.

There is no clear data supporting the notion that making shareholder value maximization the objective of the firm actually *does* maximize shareholder value over the long term. However, on the basis of the elegance of the logic, it has become the prevailing theory that governs our capital markets and business community.

The argument against shareholder value maximization works from the same critical assumption as does the theory itself: agents are self-interested and will maximize their own outcomes over and above that of shareholders. Jensen and Meckling argue that changing the rules of the game can overcome this self-interest. But they may have underestimated how hard the new rules would be for executives, and how much easier it would be for executives to "game the game" instead.

Consider the logic. Expectations race far ahead of reality, and it is not possible to beat them forever (or, really, for very long at all). The world's very best companies, whether Cisco, Microsoft, Google, Citigroup, or GE, have expectations placed on them that vastly exceed what is achievable. As a consequence, the goal of maximizing shareholder value takes on a problematic dimension for the executives charged with accomplishing it. Since they are increasingly aware that they can't keep expectations rising (let alone rising forever), executives start to play games, none of which are at all good for shareholders.

Stock-based compensation, rather than aligning their interests with shareholders, gives executives the incentive to work on causing expectations to rise in the short-term and then get out quickly in order to exploit the unsustainably high expectations. It also makes it worthwhile for executives to cause expectations to crater shortly after their appointment, giving them a long runway from which to rebuild expectations (and allowing the stock-based compensation that they receive at the bottom of the trough to soar).

Since shareholder value enhancement occurs entirely in the expectations market, executives have a powerful incentive to spend their time, energy, and efforts playing there rather than in the real market. Rather than ask, "How can I make my performance in the real market better?" they will ask, "What's best for the expectations market?" They will do so because their incentive compensation scheme demands it.

But executives have a profoundly difficult task in the expectations market. Recall that the stock price is the sum of all investors' expectations about the future performance of the company, and that those expectations are only partly tied to the company's real activities. Consider, too, how money actually flows through the capital markets. Imagine that a company went public at a price of $20 a share. At the time of that initial public offering (IPO), the company actually received and put to use all of the money that it raised in the offering—$20 times however many shares it issued. Subsequently, the company performed so well that investors' expectations increased and the company's share price rose to $100.

Now imagine further that an investor in the initial public offering decides to sell her shares to a third party at the prevailing rate of $100 a share. The company is not party to this transaction; it entirely concerns two external parties and occurs without the company's approval or consent. The company receives no benefit from the exchange, no additional capital with which to build plants, expand markets, and the like. The initial investor pockets $80 of profit, thanks to the high expectations. And where does the company find itself relative to the new investor? According to the prevailing theory, it now owes that new investor a return above the cost of equity (which we will again assume is 15 percent) on the $100 share price, even though the company only received the original $20 of equity capital. The means of producing earnings derives from the real market (the $20 per share of real investment made by the original investor), while the target for those earnings comes from the expectations market (the $100 per share stock price), a market that operates without real constraints. So now the company needs to earn 15 percent on $100 per share of expectations capital, even though it has only $20 of real capital with which to do it. Rather than a 15 percent return on its real equity (or $3/share), it has to earn a 75 percent return on its real equity (or $15/share), a deeply challenging task and one that even the best companies are unlikely to achieve over time.

The biggest downside of this real-versus-expectations split is the length executives can and will go to attempt to produce returns that will satisfy expectations. They will take excessive risks in order to attempt to meet these unattainable targets, as technology companies proved in 2000 and banks did in 2008. This pressure shortens the competitive cycles of far too many companies, as they chase market expectations while financed by much lower levels of real equity.

THE CASE AGAINST SHAREHOLDER VALUE MAXIMIZATION

The data behind the case against shareholder value maximization as the proper objective of the company are not entirely persuasive, but they are telling. To examine the data, let's compare the periods before and after the beginning of the shareholder value era.

The decades that preceded the shareholder value era were notable in that they marked the rise of the professional manager. Until the 1930s, American commerce was dominated by CEO-owners like the Rockefellers, Mellons, Carnegies, and Morgans. But during the middle of the twentieth century, firms increasingly came to be run by the hired help, a new class of professional CEOs. It was this shift that in 1976 Jensen and Meckling found so troublesome. In particular, they argued that owners were getting short shrift from these professional managers, who enhanced their own financial well-being at the expense of the shareholders in a way that an owner-manager would not have done. The result, they maintained, was that shareholders were earning a suboptimally low return on their investment because professional managers were wasting resources by padding their own bank accounts.

Were these managers extracting unreasonable sums from their companies in the period just before the rise of shareholder value theory? Interestingly, despite the intuitive appeal of this nest-feathering hypothesis, the data do not suggest that they were. One way to calibrate CEO compensation is to determine the total compensation dollars earned per dollar of net income earned by the company. The higher the resulting amount, the greater the "take" of management (represented here by the CEO) versus shareholders. Between 1960 and 1980, CEO compensation per dollar of net income earned for the 365 biggest publicly traded American companies fell by 33 percent.[12] CEOs earned more for their shareholders for steadily less and less relative compensation. These CEOs may well have been squandering company resources in other ways, but they certainly weren't utilizing their positions to extract resources out of the company and pour them into their own compensation.

But this all changed in 1980, just as Jack Welch took over GE and Roberto Goizueta became CEO of Coca-Cola. After falling steadily by one-third over the prior two decades, CEO compensation per dollar of net earnings produced doubled in the decade from 1980 to 1990. And if that wasn't enough, CEO compensation per dollar of net earnings produced *quadrupled* between 1990 and 2000—up eightfold in the two decades after shareholders supposedly wrested back the upper hand from management.[13]

On the basis of this data, it could be fairly argued that shareholders had it pretty good before the age of shareholder value capitalism, and that the advent of the shareholder value era was a boon for executives rather than for shareholders. However, if shareholders also did much better in the 1980–2000 period, the growth in CEO compensation may have been perfectly reasonable. Perhaps both boats were lifted, as the prevailing theory suggests.

Unfortunately, as pointed out in chapter 1, nothing of this sort happened. Returns to shareholders were better in the period before the shift to shareholder value capitalism than after. From the beginning of the shift to professional management, which can be marked from the publication of a seminal book by Adolf A. Berle and Gardiner C. Means called *The Modern Corporation and Private Property* in 1933, to the publication of Jensen and Meckling's article in 1976, total real compound annual return on the S&P 500 was 7.5 percent.[14] Since 1976, the total real return on the S&P 500 was 6.5 percent (compound annual).[15]

It is hard to argue that the age of shareholder value maximization worked out well for shareholders, but it is also difficult to make the case that shareholders have done definitively worse. While the difference between 7.5 percent and 6.5 percent is meaningful, especially when compounded over more than three decades, the rates of return change depending on what years and indices are measured. For instance, parity for the shareholder value age and the period before it can be achieved if the start and end dates are sufficiently manipulated. What cannot be delivered with any degree of credibility, however, is evidence that shareholders have done better after 1976 than they did before. The data just aren't there.

Looking at narrower, company-level data, one might ask: how do companies that explicitly put shareholder value theory at the heart of the strategy do relative to those who do not? As we saw earlier in this chapter, J&J clearly puts shareholders fourth in its list of priorities, well behind customers, and tells shareholders it is interested in earning only a "fair" return for them. Despite that, J&J actually beat Jack Welch at creating share-holder value, growing it at 14.5 percent compound annually versus 12.3 percent for GE over Welch's two decades as CEO.[16] Compared with another shareholder value–creation legend, Roberto Goizueta, who ran Coca-Cola from 1980 until his death in 1997, J&J did just fine too. It created value at a 15.0 percent clip versus Coca-Cola's 15.1 percent during Goizueta's 17-year tenure. Procter & Gamble, with its own clear focus on customers first, outperformed Welch 15.2 percent to 12.3 percent and, at 14.6 percent, almost equaled Goizueta's numbers.[17]

Apple Corporation provides another interesting exemplar. By happenstance, Apple was founded in 1976, the very beginning of the shareholder value era. The company had a brilliant first five years, including its 1980 IPO, which was the biggest since that of the Ford Motor Company in 1956.[18] But by 1983, prevailing wisdom dictated that the aggressive young entrepreneurs who had founded the company needed the wisdom, marketing acumen, and financial discipline of a professional manager; thus, Apple's board brought in as CEO John Sculley, the world-class marketer who had created the Pepsi Challenge while at PepsiCo. Almost immediately, there was friction between Sculley and cofounder Steve Jobs, who was subsequently sent packing.

Though Sculley was able to keep market expectations high for a number of years, he struggled to produce returns in the real market. By 1993, with Apple facing declining margins, diminishing sales and an eroding stock price, Sculley was out. And in 1997, prodigal son Jobs returned as CEO.

When Jobs returned, he had to deal with a market capitalization that had fallen to $2.1 billion, less than a quarter of its high in 1992 and almost back to the level of its IPO. Yet, within the space of thirteen years, Jobs accomplished the unthinkable. On May 26, 2010, Apple overtook Microsoft to become the most valuable technology company in the world and the second-most-valuable company—of any kind—after Exxon Mobil. It was a stunning reversal of the position of the two rivals in 1997, when Microsoft was worth forty times as much as Apple.[19] Based on Apple's market capitalization of $222 billion on May 26, 2010, Jobs had provided his 1997 shareholders with a hundred-times return on their investment, or a 43 percent compound annual growth in shareholder value over thirteen years.

A key feature of Jobs' approach as CEO has been to make clear to the shareholders where they stand: they will do well if Apple serves its customers well, and they should otherwise stay out of his face. If we are to deduce anything from his actions, his view seems to be that shareholders had no right to even be informed, let alone given details or reassurances, even when he suffered a life-threatening ailment. Shareholders objected strongly to being treated with such apparent disdain, but Jobs made no gesture in their direction other than to tell them, through the media, that his health was his business and no one else's.

Clearly, there are several ways to put shareholders behind customers on the priority list. It can be done frankly but respectfully as it is at J&J; it can be done with subtlety as it is at P&G, or it can be with seeming impudence as it is at Apple. Regardless of the approach, each company puts customers ahead of shareholders, yet each still manages to deliver strong, if not outstanding, returns to its shareholders. And each stands apart, an outlier from the mass of its competitors, all of whom embrace the prevailing theory of shareholder value maximization.

In sum, there are no obvious data to support the logic of shareholder value maximization and alignment of executive/investor interests through stock-based compensation. There are, however, some data that would argue against the adoption of the shareholder value schema: In general, shareholders did worse, not better, in the shareholder value era, and several prominent companies demonstrate that an effective route to genuinely increasing shareholder value lies in rejecting rather than embracing the prevailing theory.

THE POWERFUL OBJECTIVE

If we accept that the data as to the value of a shareholder-value orientation are at least somewhat equivocal, we must consider another way to determine which objective to optimize. To do so, it is important to consider the varied powers of different objectives. Imagine your company has a primary objective and a number of important but subordinate objectives. Ideally, your pursuit of the primary objective would help you simultaneously achieve a number of subordinate objectives. In effect, the secondary objectives turn out to be subsets of the primary objective, as if the primary objective is clay objects and the secondary objective is clay spheres. We can maximize both, because *sphere* is a subset of *object*. Such an objective is a powerful one.

A weak objective, on the other hand, is one that is at odds with other desirable outcomes—for example, where the primary objective is spheres and the secondary objective is cubes (see figure 2-2). Every time you make a cube, you are giving up the opportunity to make a sphere. The allure of the powerful objective rests on the fact that it incorporates other important goals as subsets rather than fighting against them.

Let's consider a specific example. Suppose that I am considering the following two objectives for my work life: objective one is to get ahead in my career as quickly

FIGURE 2-2

Differing objectives

A powerful objective

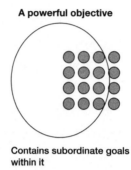

Contains subordinate goals
within it

A weak objective

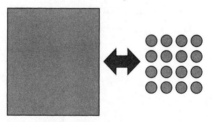

Works against subordinate goals

as possible, and objective two is to be regarded as the best possible colleague at work.

If I decide to maximize the first objective, it is likely that I will seek individual credit and trample over others or simply elbow them out of the way. There is a good chance, then, that I will be seen not as a good colleague but rather as a detestable one. So the first objective does a poor job of helping me simultaneously accomplish the second; it does not draw the second goal along in its wake.

But if I decide instead to maximize the second goal, I will be inclined to share credit, befriend my peers, and genuinely seek out the opinions of others. I will be well liked by my colleagues and, in all likelihood, still advance in the organization relatively quickly as my superiors recognize my strong interpersonal skills and identify me as someone with whom they are eager to work.

Now imagine a corporate-level choice between two goals: increasing market share over the next five years versus increasing current-year profitability. The latter goal, when placed as the overarching objective, is substantially at odds with the former. Often, the very best way to increase this year's profits is to sacrifice market share by increasing prices—and to do the same for the next year and the next. So if the company seeks to maximize annual profit repeatedly over the next five years, it will probably harvest share in each of the five years. At the end of five years, it will have significantly lower market share—although in each individual year, it will have maximized the profitability available in that particular year.

If, instead, the company seeks to maximize market share over five years, it will behave differently. It may sacrifice some profit in a given year and price aggressively to build share. But over the longer haul, as the size of the business grows with the acquisition of each new point of market share, the profit has a good chance of increasing as well, even if profit per point of share is lower. The more powerful objective helps to achieve subordinate goals as well, while the weaker objective does not. In this example, five-year share maximization is likely to be a more powerful objective than current-year profitability.

So which is the most powerful maximizing objective—placing shareholders first or placing customers first? Is the maximization of shareholder value the most powerful goal, one that draws along with it many other objectives we'd wish to achieve, or a weaker one that actually works against our other objectives?

To assess that question, it is important to understand what we want of our executives. One could argue that we want them to make money for their investors, but also to treat their employees well (especially if we are among them), to play fair with their customers, to compete in their industry with integrity, and to manage our environment with respect and care. Among these subordinate goals, none are particularly well aligned with the goal of maximizing shareholder value. To maximize shareholder value, an executive would be inclined to do all he can to keep employee wages and benefits low, take advantage of naive customers, collude with the competition to exploit the consumer, and think little of the environment, if at all. In a short-run, zero-sum game, self-interest would prevail.

Consider, on the other hand, placing the customer's interests at the heart of the company's goals. Then, employees—who are often customers, too—become far more important. An executive would be more inclined to treat employees as he wants them to treat his customers. Fair competition would be encouraged, insofar as it creates greater choice and happier consumers. The environment would be protected, again insofar as it matters to customers. Finally, with happy customers come greater profits and greater returns for shareholders. In each case, the subordinate goals are far more closely aligned to the primacy of customers than of shareholders.

THE NFL OUTPERFORMS AGAIN

Once again, the NFL provides a sterling example of the success of a powerful objective. We have already seen that the NFL completely sequesters the expectations and real markets by prohibiting any insider involvement in sports betting. But in addition, the league has made it consistently clear that the singular focus of the real game is on the fans, rather than the owners. Job number one has been to put a product on the field that is maximally enjoyable and stimulating for its customers. The logic is that if the NFL accomplishes that goal on an ongoing basis, the owners will be just fine.

The job of an individual owner is to develop a local fan base over time by building a team, connecting with the community, providing an enjoyable stadium experience, and winning football games (rather than beating the point spread). At the macro level, the NFL commissioner's office, as the moral equivalent of the league's primary regulator, is responsible for creating a structure that enables all of the teams to thrive, and it does so through a relentless focus on the fan experience.

The NFL has engaged in a continuous, decades-long effort to tweak the economics off the field and competitive play on the field to steadily build the game. This effort is in stark contrast to American capitalism, where there is a prevailing view that the capital markets represent the last bastion of economic freedom in America and so shouldn't be meddled with. Capital markets cowboys are allowed to roam free and game the system for their own benefit—until a massive crash leads to dramatic, wholesale regulatory change, which the cowboys then work to their own advantage again, leading to the next big crash. In contrast, the NFL watches and listens—and tweaks, and tweaks, and tweaks.

As the NFL grew into a truly big-money sport in the late 1970s and early 1980s, it withstood a series of damaging fights with its players, including a 1982 strike that reduced the season from sixteen games to nine and a 1987 lockout, when the league used replacement players for three games and cancelled one game. The league endured the labor strife and fought hard for a salary cap, revenue sharing, and a free-agency system that would enable small-market franchises like the Green Bay Packers to compete with big-city clubs in New York, Dallas, and Miami.[20]

The salary cap puts a ceiling on the amount each team is allowed to spend on its roster of players. Combined with revenue sharing from lucrative television contracts, which gives each team enough money to spend up to its salary cap, this creates economic parity among teams. The NFL's is by no means either the first or only salary cap. The National Basketball Association had a cap in place in 1984, a decade before the NFL (1994). But the NBA cap is a "soft" cap, with all sorts of exceptions that enable the rich teams, like the New York Knicks and Los Angeles Lakers, to outspend poorer teams. The NFL's cap is rigid and rigorously enforced, which gives all teams the capacity to compete. Major League Baseball, on the other hand, has no salary cap, which makes the big-spending New York Yankees the perennial favorite to win the World Series.[21]

The NFL also tweaked the free-agency system to make sure that teams losing free-agent players to another team would be compensated with valuable draft picks, mitigating the effect of the talent loss. It is the most meaningful and impactful free-agent compensation system among the major professional sports.

Together, the salary cap, revenue sharing (including new stadium opportunities), and the free-agent compensation system are fan-focused measures designed to ensure that every team has a chance of building a winner. These three measures represent a clear focus on the customer, rather than on the individual owner, and impressive commitment to the fan experience. Relative parity of teams is important because teams that lose consistently do little for fan excitement or engagement. A team can lose in the short term, but there must be some possibility that, under good management, it can win in the future. It is a tribute to the management of parity by the league that teams like the New England Patriots and New Orleans Saints have been able to go from perennial doormats to Super Bowl Champions.

But more impressive still has been the NFL's continuous tweaking of the rules of competition to ensure a balance between offense and defense, with the aim of giving fans exciting and unpredictable games. This balance is critical: if the team on the offense will almost surely be trumped by the defense every time, fans will lose interest; if it is a foregone conclusion that the offense will triumph over the defense, fans will again tune out.

In sports, as strategies change and the skills of players increase over time, advantage can tilt one way or the other. Men's soccer is dangerously close to the utter dominance of defense over offense, which has almost certainly constrained the growth of professional soccer in America. In six-man hard-court volleyball, offenses now have the clear upper hand on defenses, which has contributed to the sport's decline in popularity, fan interest, and commercial viability relative to its fast-growing sister sport, two-man beach volleyball, in which offense is more balanced with defense.

The NFL's competition committee recognizes this pattern. It sees that a smart head coach will attempt to game the game to his advantage; while that kind of advance can bring change and excitement to the sport for a time, it can also unbalance it and damage the fan experience over a longer timeframe. As a result, the league has played a cat-and-mouse game whereby advantages are given to the offense when defensive innovation threatens it and vice versa.

A case in point: in 1979, a college football coach named Bill Walsh took over the hapless San Francisco 49ers, whose record of two wins and fourteen losses in 1978 made it the laughingstock of the NFL. In his first year as head coach, as Walsh took stock of the miserable team he had inherited, the team again racked up fourteen losses. But at the end of the 1979 season, he decided to implement an entirely new offensive regime. In the third round of that year's college draft, Walsh selected from Notre Dame a weak-armed but quick-thinking quarterback named Joe Montana to run his new offense.

Walsh's scheme, which is now famously called the *West Coast Offense*, involved marching down the field throwing short passes—three- or four-yard passes to receivers crossing the field in front of the quarterback—rather than using the traditional mix of running the ball and throwing long passes of ten yards or more downfield. Ten-yard passes are inherently attractive because each team has only four attempts to move the ball ten yards down field. If the team succeeds, it retains possession of the ball and gets another four attempts for the next ten yards and so on until it eventually scores (or fails and turns the ball over to the other team). Teams had traditionally focused on long passes, because they held the promise of "moving the sticks" (or getting first down yardage) in a single play. In contrast, Walsh's short passes were *high-percentage* plays, more likely to be completed successfully than riskier long passes, and when strung together were more likely to earn successive first downs and march his team down the field to score. The strategy was tremendously productive.

On the back of his new West Coast Offense, Walsh turned a 2-and-14 team into a Super Bowl champion in just two years. The 49ers won the Super Bowl in 1981,

1984, and again in 1988. Walsh retired after the 1988 Super Bowl victory and turned over the team to George Seifert, his second-in-command, who led the team to another Super Bowl victory in 1989—an amazing total of four championships in nine years in a parity-obsessed league. The "weak-armed" Montana is now in the NFL Hall of Fame and is considered by many to be the greatest quarterback to ever play the game.[22]

Meanwhile, Commissioner Pete Rozelle watched what the West Coast Offense was doing to the balance between offense and defense, waiting to see what would unfold as the rest of the league reacted to the innovation. Walsh had found a clever way for offense to get the upper hand. As is often the case, there was soon a competitive reaction to Walsh's new strategy: Defensive backs, the players primarily tasked with defending against passes, got bigger and stronger (and richer) as defensive coordinators tried to do whatever they could to stop the offense from completing a succession of short passes. These bigger, stronger defensive backs attempted to jostle, intimidate, and out-position the receivers to break up the rhythm of the offense. The market reaction was helpful, but it was not enough to rebalance things sufficiently, so Rozelle decided to act. To restore balance, the NFL tweaked both the rules and the official interpretation of them. Previously, defensive backs were not allowed to contact the receiver prior to the receiver catching the ball. The rules changed to allow defensive backs to hit (or "chuck," in NFL vernacular) the receivers once in the first five yards from the line of scrimmage, making it less likely that the quarterback would find the receiver where he expected him to be and thus make it more difficult to complete the quick, short passes. Perhaps more importantly, over the 1980s and early 1990s, referees became ever more liberal in allowing defensive backs to impede the receivers—all in an effort to limit the effectiveness of the West Coast Offense.

Just as these changes were being implemented, innovative coaches were creating new ways to game the game. A new form of linebacker (the intermediate-sized defenders who work between the giant defensive linemen and the smaller and quicker defensive backs) was emerging, and defensive coaching genius Bill Parcells, who might be called the anti-Walsh, put them to very good use. Utilizing players who were big, brutish, and out for blood, Parcells pioneered a linebacker-centric defense that created chaos for offenses by relentlessly "blitzing" the quarterback (that is, crossing the line of scrimmage to attempt to tackle to quarterback). This new scheme interrupted the offensive passing game and turned the tide in favor of the defense. Led by Lawrence Taylor—whose game-changing career serves as the opening note to the Oscar-winning movie *The Blind Side*—Parcells's defensive-powerhouse New York

Giants won Super Bowl Championships in 1987 and 1991.[23]

Between Rozelle's rule changes and Parcells's innovations, defense now had the upper hand. So, Rozelle's successor Paul Tagliabue went to his mentor's playbook and started tweaking. Defensive backs were reined in to free up receivers to run their routes. Offensive linemen were given more freedom to use their arms to slow blitzing defenders. Quarterbacks were protected from blows to head, leg shots, and hits after they released the ball on passing plays. As a result, balance was restored.

By keeping the NFL entrenched in the real game, Rozelle and his successors kept the league focused first and foremost on the fans; they continually tweaked the game so as to delight their customers and build the league slowly but surely. The NFL does not seek to make life wonderful for bettors and bookmakers, especially when doing so negatively influences the fan experience. Yet it doesn't ignore the gamblers entirely, recognizing that they are a reality of football life and important to some fans. The league forces teams to disclose player injuries and categorize those with injuries as either *out*, *doubtful*, *questionable*, or *probable* to play, which is largely for the utility of football's expectations market.

The NFL leadership has always understood that if it focuses on the fans and tweaks the product with the customer in mind, it will produce lots of value for the owners—the J&J model as applied to professional sports. *Forbes* values the teams in the NFL at $33 billion, collectively, up almost three times from $12 billion a decade ago. With fans and the real game as the focus, owners have indeed done just fine.[24]

LESSONS FOR AMERICAN CAPITALISM

American capitalism should learn an important lesson from the NFL. We've already seen that it would be wise to echo the NFL's isolation of the game played on the field—the real game—from the unhelpful entanglements of betting on that game—the expectations market. Now the lesson is to put customers clearly and unambiguously first—maximize their delight in the real game—and trust that owners will still make a tidy return.

The prevailing theory holds that it is the obligation of a business to maximize its return to shareholders rather than to focus on delivering customer value. But the example of the NFL, in addition to the examples of J&J, P&G, and Apple, suggests another choice, one that goes beyond even customer value; a company can choose to attempt to maximize customer delight through the creation of products, services, and experiences that exceed basic expectations and deliver genuine joy. Maximizing customer delight is a powerful objective that embodies many other worthwhile goals, including employee happiness and shareholder value. In this way, it is an integrative solution that actually obviates the need to choose between customers and shareholders. Choosing customer delight enables an organization to satisfy them both.

In order to maximize customer delight, those responsible for regulating American capitalism must recognize that we will have to keep tweaking the game; otherwise, savvy players will inevitably game the game in ways that diminish the customer experience. It is not possible to "get it right and leave it alone." In particular, there will always be attempts by capital markets intermediaries and their friends to enable the expectations market to penetrate the real market. In this regard, tweaks are already necessary.

An example is the 1995 Private Securities Litigation Reform Act, which contains what has become known to anyone who has participated in an earnings release presentation as the *safe harbor provision*. This provision protects company executives who offer earnings guidance to investors, enabling them to provide that guidance without fear of getting into trouble or being held accountable for it. Citing the safe harbor provision before making their presentation authorizes them to use "forward-looking" weasel-words such as *anticipating, projecting, expecting*, and *estimating* to make predictions of future performance, and to be protected from lawsuits when their predictions are found to be off base. This provision plainly encourages and facilitates the penetration of the expectations market into the real market by giving executives a powerful tool for expectations manipulation. To move ahead productively, the safe harbor provision should simply be repealed. Executives and their companies should be legally liable for any attempt to manage expectations. Without the safe harbor provisions, there would be no earnings guidance and that would be a great thing.

Similarly, the application of FASB 142 to determine goodwill impairment represents another incursion by the expectations market into the real market. Because auditors can force the real write-downs of real assets based on the company's share price in the expectations market, executives must concern themselves unhelpfully with managing expectations in order to avoid write-downs. FASB should mandate that impairment calculations use only real-market measures—such as estimated discounted cash flow relative to real assets rather than to share price.

American capitalism needs the moral equivalent of an NFL commissioner to weed out existing incursions of the expectations market into the real market—like the safe harbor provision and FASB 142—and to guard against any new attempted incursions. And, as with the NFL, customers should be the commissioner's dominant concern, because it is real-market customers who need protection. When the expectations market infil-trates the real market, customers suffer. As with the NFL, investors (bettors) and capital market intermediaries (bookies) don't need to be coddled and treated as if they are the center of the universe. If executives focus on the real market, investors will do just fine. Capital market intermediaries will, as they always have, look after themselves and so don't need special protection and care. They will attempt to game the game for their own purposes and thus the rules will need to be tweaked, as in the NFL, to make sure the game isn't gamed to death.

To help companies focus on maximizing customer delight rather than shareholder value, we should fundamentally redefine the obligation of the company relative to its shareholders. Currently, the obligation is to maximize shareholder value, defined as increasing the share price from its current level to the maximum extent possible. This obligation should be changed to one consistent with the J&J credo, which is that shareholders should realize a "fair return."

Further, a company should feel obligated only to earn a return on the equity that shareholders actually gave to the company, plus the real earnings that the company chooses to reinvest, rather than pay out to shareholders by way of dividends. The goal should be to earn a return that is above investors' risk-adjusted cost of equity, not a return at the highest level possible. This shift is critically important because every company needs capital to invest in maintaining its competitive position. The fundamental problem for highly successful companies is that their success sends their expectations soaring. As expectations rise, investors sell shares between themselves, enriching each other but not providing an additional cent of capital to the company. When expectations get sufficiently high, the company's ability to invest in maintaining or growing the competitive advantage that fed those high expectations in the first place is massively constrained.

As of July 2010, Google was trading at a market-to-book ratio of its equity of four times. Imagine we were to argue that its required rate of return on equity is 10 percent. Using book equity, Google looks pretty good, making a 20 percent return. However, a market-to-book ratio of four times means that Google needs to make a return of 40 percent on book equity to achieve a 10 percent return on market equity. Google, despite being one of the most dynamic and admired companies on the planet, is failing its shareholders according to the prevailing theory.

The theory must be changed, and companies must be under no legal or regulatory obligation to earn a return on anything but the equity they have been given and the earnings they have retained—that is, capital from the real market to be used in the real market.[25] Only if they are freed from expectations market–generated return targets will successful companies be able to invest for the long term in delighting customers.

In the end, the goal of achieving customer delight is to turn companies from attending in vain to the expectations market to attending to the real market and to customers in that market. Tending to the real market will provide a greater ability to extend and expand a company's competitive position and enable the investments necessary to do so. The message is clear: customer delight is a more powerful objective than shareholder value. As J&J, P&G, Apple, and the NFL so aptly demonstrate, if you take care of customers, shareholders will be drawn along for a very nice ride. The opposite is simply not true: if you try to take care of shareholders, customers don't benefit and, ironically, shareholders don't get very far either.

THREE

RESTORING EXECUTIVE AUTHENTICITY

To thine own self be true, and it must follow,
as the night the day, thou cans't not then be false
to any man.

—William Shakespeare, *Hamlet*

Management Science is a prestigious top-tier academic journal, the kind in which business academics strive to be published, especially as they work toward gaining tenure. A typical issue might feature original research in behavioral economics, competitive dynamics, or game theory. As with other top-tier journals, the articles tend to be written in dense "academese," and require a rich background in statistics and mathematics to be understood. With a paid circulation of just five thousand, its publication doesn't typically cause much of a stir outside the walls of business academia.[1]

Minuscule circulation notwithstanding, the May 2005 issue of *Management Science* included an article that would go on to have wide-reaching and dramatic effects on our world. "On the Timing of CEO Stock Option Awards" was written by Erik Lie, an associate professor of finance at the Tippie College of Business at the University of Iowa.[2] Lie was then a relatively unknown young academic, in the first decade of his career and with only two prior top-tier journal articles to his name. But that was about to change.

THE OPTIONS BACKDATING SAGA

Erik Lie's article summarized his study of CEO stock option awards from 1992 through 2002. In particular, it analyzed a large data set of 1,668 "unscheduled" awards during that period. Lie had studied options awarded by boards of directors to CEOs outside of structured, contractual agreements, so excluded options that were awarded on a regular schedule, such as those made annually on January 1. In essence, Lie looked only at those instances when the board patted the CEO on the head and said, "Here are some stock options for your good work."

Such options are typically granted at market price on the day of the award. That's because if options were awarded below the market price, they would be deemed to contain a capital gain and the CEO would face an immediate tax bill. If, alternatively, they were granted above market price, the stock price would have to rise just to make them worth anything at all. So the norm was, and remains, to issue stock options at the market price on the day the award is made. This was putatively the case for every one of the 1,668 awards Lie examined.

In 1997, David Yermack at the Stern School at NYU had published a paper in the *Journal of Finance* (another prestigious academic journal) showing that stock prices tend to increase shortly after option grants—a suspicious finding but not one that created much of a stir.[3] Lie wanted to dig deeper, and so set out to look at the period both before and after the grant date to see whether there was a suspicious drop prior to the option date and further evidence of Yermack's suspicious rise afterward. Across a data set as big as Lie's, one would expect to find no particular pattern, but rather a random distribution in which some stock prices went up before issue and down after, some went down before the issue and up after, some continued on a downward path irrespective of the issue, and some went up before the issue and up again after. Lie wanted to examine whether movements of the stock were indeed random or, as Yermack's paper had suggested, abnormal.

Lie's results were nothing short of stunning. Across his sample, prices seemed to mysteriously fall just before unscheduled CEO stock option grants. In the thirty days leading up to the option grant, there was a 3 percent abnormal decline, most of which happened in the final ten days before the award. But rather than continue to fall, prices miraculously reversed course after the grant award, showing an abnormal gain of 2 percent in the first ten days and another 2 percent in the following twenty days. Think of a V-shaped curve in a stock price chart over time; Lie found that stock options were consistently granted right at the bottom of the V (see figure 3-1).

The likelihood of finding V-shaped patterns on a historical stock chart is almost 100 percent; such a pattern

FIGURE 3-1

V-shaped patterns on a stock chart

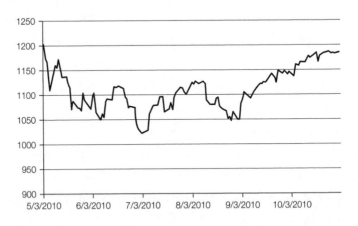

Source: This chart uses six months of daily returns for the S&P 500.

Note the series of V-shaped patterns as the index changes direction.

emerges whenever a stock changes direction, stopping a downward decline and heading back up. However, the chance of options consistently being granted at the very bottom of the V randomly, naturally, or as the result of an eerily prescient board is infinitesimally small, not to mention wonderfully beneficial for the recipient of the option. In fact, Lie's work shows beyond a shadow of a doubt that the pattern of awards could *not* be random.

How was it, then, that options grants were made consistently at the lowest stock price in the sixty-day period beginning thirty days before the award? It turns out that the options were *backdated*. A board would decide to award options to a well-performing executive on, for example, March 17. Then somebody, whether CEO, CFO, EVP-HR, or corporate secretary, would pore over the stock movements for the previous several months and find the day the stock price was at its lowest point, say February 24. The company would then enter into the corporate records that the options award was made on February 24, the bottom-of-the-V day, rather than on March 17; in other words, the award would be backdated from March 17 to February 24. At the time, Lie estimated that a full 23 percent of the unscheduled grants were backdated. The problem? While options backdating was technically legal (if the executive in question declared and paid tax on the capital gain that occurred upon the award of an "in-the-money" option), lying about it most assuredly was not. In essence, though he was careful not to say so explicitly, Lie had found 384 acts of securities and accounting fraud.

Despite *Management Science*'s relative obscurity outside business schools, Lie's article soon came to the attention of authorities at the Securities and Exchange Commission (SEC). Within his overall data set, Lie could pinpoint the specific companies and grants that were most abnormal, so it was a treasure trove for SEC investigators. Within six months, the *Wall Street Journal* broke the story of the SEC investigation.[4]

Suddenly, options backdating was front-page news and Erik Lie very famous. In 2007, *Time* magazine named him one of the world's one hundred most influential people, along with Barack Obama, Oprah Winfrey, Richard Branson, and Steve Jobs.[5] In the same year, *BusinessWeek* named him one of the ten most influential business professors in the world.[6] And in 2008, the Tippie School promoted him to a full, chaired professorship.

Lie deserved the acclaim; he had uncovered a significant scandal, the meaning and scope of which was truly stunning. A subsequent Lie study, published in 2009, showed that some 29 percent of American businesses that made stock option grants to executives from 1995 to 2006 had manipulated them. That's two thousand companies engaging in suspect behavior.[7] Backdating options was dubious at many levels: options backdating defrauds shareholders by enriching executives at the investors' expense; it constitutes unambiguous corporate accounting fraud; and it aids and abets personal tax fraud for the individual executives. Malfeasance on this scale does not happen accidentally; you don't find the precise bottom of the V without crystal clear intent. It takes a conspiracy—a CEO and CFO and sometimes others working together. In the end, more than one hundred companies, including dozens from Silicon Valley and leading firms like Dell, Apple, Broadcom, and United Health, were scrutinized by the SEC. Eventually, some 150 companies issued restatements related to options backdating. Numerous executives were fired, many were banned from serving as corporate officers, some were fined, and at least five went to prison.[8]

It was one more case of executives behaving badly. The options backdating scandal was not the only corporate scandal of the first decade of the new century. The accounting scandal that ensnared Enron, WorldCom, and others also sent senior executives to prison for long sentences. In fact, within an eight-year period we witnessed three massive, blowout scandals involving hundreds of executives each: the accounting scandals (2001–2002), the options backdating scandal (2005–2006), and the subprime mortgage scandal (2008–2009). As a result, the reputation of corporate executives took a pounding. In a 2010 Gallup poll rating of the perceived ethical standards of people in different professions, business executives ranked just a few notches above car salesmen and below lawyers. Just 15 percent of respondents rated the honesty and ethical standards of business executives as high or very high; by contrast, nurses were well regarded by 81 percent of respondents.[9]

The illegal and unethical behavior of business executives over the past few decades suggests that something is seriously out of whack in the corporate world. Assuming that people would rather be ethical than unethical, how did we wind up with such pervasive unethical and illegal behavior? How is it that executives have come to act in ways that are so much at odds with what we would expect of them—and of what they should expect of themselves? They have fallen down the proverbial slippery slope, pushed by perverse incentives to behave in ways that are less and less ethical, more and more inauthentic.

Admittedly, not all executives deserve to be tarred for the failings of a few, or even a few thousand. Not all executives engaged in the activities that led to the scandals of the past decade. But many do engage in a practice that exists right at the precipice of the slippery slope, one that skates very close to the line of illegality and betrays the spirit of securities laws and accounting regulations: earnings management.

THE DAWN OF EARNINGS MANAGEMENT

In an article in the *Journal of Accounting and Economics*—yet another top-tier journal—Eli Bartov, Dan Givoly, and Carla Hayn showed that, regardless of the level of performance, a company's stock performs better if the company meets or beats analyst earnings expectations.[10] That is, a company is likely to see its stock perform better if it earns $1.10 per share when its consensus estimate was $1.08 per share than if it earns $1.12 per share when the consensus estimate was $1.15 per share. Superior relative performance in the expectations market (+2¢ versus –3¢) trumps absolutely better performance in the real market ($1.12 versus $1.10).

The motivation to meet the numbers by any means necessary is clear, and the means, increasingly, is earnings management. *Earnings management*, in this context, means tailoring returns to meet market expectations rather than to reflect actual performance. This approach takes two primary forms: accounting manipulations and expectations management.

In accounting manipulations, a firm fudges its financial statements to adjust earnings artificially, typically inflating them, to meet expectations. This might take the form of accounting for sales in the current quarter that really should go into the next, shifting expenses in the opposite direction, or finding a way to hide those expenses entirely. Such earnings manipulation through accounting is a risky game, one that recently got Dell into trouble. Dell was accused of manipulating the way in which it accounted for the payments it received from Intel to buy Intel chips instead of Advanced Micro Devices chips. Putting aside whether it was morally dubious to accept the payments in the first place, the key allegation was that Dell recorded the payments in such a way as to produce the quarterly earnings analysts expected between 2002 and 2006. Although it denied any wrongdoing, Dell agreed to pay a $100 million fine, and Michael Dell, former CEO Kevin Rollins, and former CFO James Schneider all paid multimillion dollar personal fines as part of the settlement.[11] Yet, despite the risk, companies continue to engage in accounting manipulations because the rewards of meeting expectations are so clear.

The other way to manipulate earnings is to attempt to directly alter analyst expectations—that is, to "talk the analysts down" to earnings forecast levels that the company can realistically achieve. In essence, the company attempts to convince analysts that the company will not be as successful as the analysts currently believe it will be, stopping just short of actually declaring that the company will not meet the targets. As long as the information provided is shared equally with everyone, such a practice is not illegal. However, it is hardly in the category of activities designed to improve company competitiveness over time.

Bartov, Givoly, and Hayn found that as executives became more aware of stock price dynamics, they became more proficient at earnings management. In the period from 1983 to 1993, companies met or beat earnings expectations 50 percent of the time—what one might expect from a random system. But by the 1994–1997 period, companies were able to meet or exceed expectations almost 70 percent of the time, a dramatic improvement and the outcome of extreme determination, greater skill in earnings manipulation, or both.[12]

In the shareholder value era, some very prominent companies have done even better than their peers at meeting or beating expectations. As Michael Jensen has pointed out, during the heart of the Jack Welch era, GE met or beat analysts' forecasts in forty-six of forty-eight quarters between December 31, 1989, and September 30, 2001—a 96 percent hit rate. Even more impressively, in forty-one of those forty-six quarters, GE hit the analyst forecast to the *exact penny*—89 percent perfection. And in the remaining seven imperfect quarters, the tolerance was startlingly narrow: four times GE beat the projection by 2 cents, once it beat it by 1 cent, once it missed by 1 cent, and once by 2 cents. Looking at these twelve years of unnatural precision, Jensen asks rhetorically: "What is the chance that could happen if earnings were not being 'managed'?"[13] Another expectations-meeting star, Microsoft, met or beat expectations for forty-one of the first forty-two quarters after it went public in 1986—its only glitch being a miss by one penny in 1988. Justin Fox, author of the *Fortune* article that noted this trend, argued that Microsoft managed this near-perfect record by accounting for revenue in a way that "virtually no other software company does."[14] In short, the likelihood of real performance driving the kind of precision seen at GE and Microsoft is infinitesimal.

Both Microsoft and GE are capable of performing very well in the real market; but the unnatural precision of their earnings suggests that the expectations market came to loom large in their boardrooms and executive suites and that expectations management became just as important, if not more so, than real performance. So, they became expert at gaming the game.

Over time, regulators have attempted to decrease the ability of companies to use games (especially accounting games) to manage earnings, through legislation, including Sarbanes-Oxley. And, indeed when John Graham, Campbell Harvey, and Shiva Rajgopal explored (again in the *Journal of Accounting and Economics*) how four hundred financial executives from major American public companies operated in the new tightened accounting environment, they found that the executives were loath to use accounting measures to smooth earnings. However, the authors also made the following worrisome discovery: "The majority of managers would avoid initiating a positive NPV [net present value] project if it meant falling short of the current quarter's consensus earnings. Similarly, more than three-fourths of the surveyed executives would give up economic value in exchange for smooth earnings."[15] That is to say, these financial executives would damage the future prospects of their company—to the clear detriment of shareholders—in order to please those same shareholders by ensuring that they unfailingly meet or beat analyst expectations. Not only have executives used accounting manipulations and talked down their own stock to meet expectations, they are willing to sacrifice the long-term financial performance of their companies in the real market in order to satisfy the vagaries of the expectations market in the short term.

In summary, then, three decades into the age of shareholder value, we have reached the point where a majority of executives freely admit to sacrificing the future of their companies in order to meet the whims of the expectations market, and in which we have suffered successive business scandals wherein hundreds of executives engaged in entirely illegal activities. In both cases, shareholders are substantially hurt rather than helped.

Earnings management is the first step down a dangerous path, yet it has become an almost universally accepted practice. That being the case, CEOs (and other executives, to be fair) now live in an unhealthy community, one that causes them to lead an inauthentic life and lose touch with their moral compass. And so we see CEOs using their talents and corporate resources to smooth earnings rather than to build their companies. And, over time, accounting and securities fraud, even on the largest scale, is no longer off limits.

THE ROLE OF COMMUNITY

Community is incredibly important in our lives. At our core, we are all social creatures who derive pleasure from the company, love, and recognition of others. Mother Teresa once said that one of humanity's greatest diseases was "to be nobody to anybody." We strive to make our mark on the world and to feel that our lives are worthwhile. The work we do is a critical component of our legacy. If we believe that our work has meaning and that we are valued by others for what we do, we are encouraged and motivated. We persevere. Even when humans engage in profoundly antisocial activities, they often do so in tightly knit social groups, whether they happen to be called Crips, Yakuza, or Al Qaeda. As social creatures, much of our happiness is derived from our relationship with a community, however that community is defined.

There are three elements to our relationship with a community that centrally determine our level of happiness: (1) our perceived value in the eyes of the community in question; (2) how much we value that community; and (3) the degree to which that community is valued by those outside it. These three elements work together to reinforce or diminish our happiness.

How does this work? Imagine that a person feels valued and appreciated by her community. That makes her happy. However, her degree of happiness will be a function of how much she cares about that community. Just as Groucho Marx slyly opined that he would never want to be a member of a club that would have him as a member, it follows that, if a person puts low value on a particular community, the esteem of that community would have less effect on her happiness than would the esteem of a community she highly values. Finally, if she is valued by the community and values it back, but the rest of the world has little regard for that community, her happiness similarly is constrained (see figure 3-2).

To return once again to the NFL for an example, when it comes to community, quarterback Drew Brees has reasons to be happy. He is valued by his community: as the starting quarterback of the New Orleans Saints, he's paid roughly $10 million per season and respected by his fellow players and his coaches. Among the many superlatives thrown at Brees by his Saints peers was

FIGURE 3-2

The happiness equation

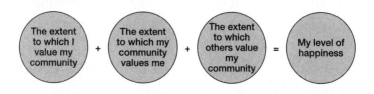

defensive back Darren Sharper's observation that Brees is "the best leader I've ever been around."[16] Brees also values his community: he chose to play for the Saints rather than the Miami Dolphins or elsewhere when he signed as a free agent in 2006, and he's seen firsthand the resurrection of New Orleans post-Katrina, which coincided with the dramatic rise in the Saints' fortunes. Coming back from a devastating shoulder injury the year before he joined the Saints, Brees knows all too well how easily it could all be taken away. Finally, he knows just how much others value his organization: He faces a crush of rabid and devoted fans before, during, and after every game. Fans and media across the country think the New Orleans Saints are a fantastic football team— and they are right: the Saints won the Super Bowl in February 2010, and Brees was named the game's MVP. He was subsequently named *Sports Illustrated* magazine's 2010 sportsman of the year. For Brees, the three drivers of happiness reinforce one another perfectly.[17]

Unlike Brees and other star athletes, Crips, Yakuza, and Al Qaeda members don't have a perfectly reinforcing happiness equation. Consider them medium-happy, because they only have two aspects of the happiness trinity working for them: while they are valued members of a community, and they value that community deeply, most people outside their community think they should be hunted down and jailed or executed. Total potential happiness is therefore reduced.

This happiness equation can change over time. For instance, our value in a community is not static. We can take actions to improve or diminish our standing. Think back to high school and recall the lengths people will go to improve their standing in a group. People will change what they do, how they do it, who they interact with, and even their whole worldview. But such change is often an unhealthy one; it may lead to greater acceptance by the community but also to dramatically reduced authenticity on the part of the individual.

AUTHENTICITY

Authenticity is the degree to which one stays true to one's own character and morals while dealing with external forces. In an ideal world, we can find communities that value us for who we are and thus allow us to act authentically and honestly within them. And, where we interact

103

with a number of communities at once, those communities would ideally be mutually reinforcing rather than at odds with one another, enabling us to be true to ourselves and consistent across contexts.

If, as was suggested earlier, we can assume that people in general would rather be good than bad, honest than dishonest, and authentic rather than inauthentic, we would want the communities in which we live to foster these instincts. Such a community could be described as a healthy one. While there are many ways to describe a healthy community, most would agree that a healthy community would:

- Believe in long-term relationships rather than one-off transactions

- Seek reciprocity rather than exploitation

- Protect its weakest members rather than gouging them

- Worry about the externalities that it creates rather than turning a blind eye to them

- Discourage member actions that endanger the community rather than encouraging them

Before the advent of shareholder value theory, the CEO's community was relatively healthy. Customers, employees, the home city of his company, and his long-term shareholders loomed large in the typical CEO community of the 1950s and 1960s. The intimacy of these relationships was aided by the scale of the enterprises of the day. GM, the only real behemoth of 1960, pulled in revenues that, even when converted to today's dollars (approximately $66 billion), would be dwarfed by Walmart's $408 billion and would barely rank in the top one hundred companies by revenues.[18]

This smaller scale meant that customers tended to be concentrated in a company's home region (or, for the largest companies, home country). So, it was relatively easy for a CEO to get to know customers, figure out how to serve them, and continuously improve products or services with those customers in mind. It was also possible to connect directly with employees, because there weren't all that many of them and they mainly lived nearby, with roots in the same home city. The executive typically lived in and had a network of friends in that city too, creating a deep link between his corporate role and his personal life. That is to say, doing things to benefit the city made sense both corporately and personally. On top of that, shareholders were likely to encourage, or at least tolerate, long-term planning as opposed to very short-term results, because shareholders planned to be around for the long term too. The relationship between corporation and shareholder was like a marriage—a partnership not without its bumps, but one in which both parties were willing to commit for the long haul.

Picture an executive of Boeing Corporation in post–World War II America. He (and they were all *he*'s then) would be pretty happy, according to our three-pronged happiness equation. He would, by dint if his status and rewards, feel that he was a valuable member of the Boeing senior management team. Since Boeing was a highly successful corporation that had materially helped the Allies win the war, he would feel pride at being part of that team. Finally, he would bask in the glory of Americans writ large, feeling that Boeing was a great company, a technology leader, and one of the country's biggest exporters. He would likely be a pillar of the Seattle community, known throughout his city as a successful Boeing executive. And even though William Boeing, the beloved founder, had sold his stake in 1934, the executive still would likely feel a sense of community with the long-standing shareholders of Boeing. When he went to work, he could feel pride in doing a great job for his team, his city, his customers, and his shareholders—together, these stakeholders created a community of which he could genuinely feel a valued part.

While not perfect, this structure enabled the executive to live a reasonably authentic life; the way he wanted to live personally was largely aligned with his corporate responsibilities. He wanted to make the customers—whom he was likely to know personally—happy. He wanted to support the well-being of his employees—many of whom he and his family knew well. He wanted to be a respected figure in the city—a city that was important to his company and his family. And he wanted to make his shareholders happy because he knew that those shareholders had placed a long-term bet behind his company. If he worked hard on all those aspects of his community, he could be successful and happy, and the corporation was likely to continue to prosper too.

Since the 1970s, as companies have ballooned in size, the CEO's traditional community has become far more distant and impersonal. Customers and employees are more dispersed (and anonymous), and the home city is far less central—even expendable. With the rise of institutional investors and mutual fund companies, a veil has been placed between the company and its shareholders. CEOs don't even know, generally, who their shareholders really are; they see only the entity that is investing the shareholders' money. All of this has weakened the bonds between the traditional community and the CEO.

Moreover, the rise of shareholder capitalism has pushed another community to the fore—the expectations market. Institutional investors, equity analysts, investment bankers, hedge funds, and the financial press have emerged as the central figures in the CEO's community. Unlike the traditional, positively reinforcing community of yore, this new community is less than healthy. Instead, it is a community rife with transactional relationships, exploitation, and distrust. Its members prey on one another, ignoring the ill effects of their actions and encouraging each other's bad behavior.

The modern institutional investor is a rational, cold-hearted (and even computerized) beast, in and out of a given stock at a whim. Yes, some investors still engage in relationship investing, but that is not the norm. But institutional investors can and do sell without warning or explanation, looking for short-term advantage and maximum profits right now. Rather than a healthy marriage, the investor-company relationship is now more akin to anonymous sex.

Equity analysts are paid to play the game of helping create a convergence between their estimates and company performance. They and everybody else involved know that if they were capable of discerning whether a stock is overvalued or undervalued even 51 percent of the time, they would be principal investors, not equity analysts, and they would be wildly rich. Instead, most analysts merely attempt to avoid looking bad, relying closely on company guidance and rewarding those companies that make them look good by meeting the agreed-upon predictions. They coo with approval when companies put shareholder value first and spank them when they don't. They dance the dance described and documented empirically by Bartov, Givoly, and Hayn, whereby they set expectations high at the beginning of a quarter and then lower them later in the quarter under pressure from the company and in a desire not to look silly.[19] It is all a game.

Wall Street investment bankers, ever on the hunt for fees, tout "value-accretive merger and acquisition ideas" sure to "enhance shareholder value." Yet they don't share in the outcome of these mergers; they take an upfront fee and walk away, unaffected by the success or failure of the enterprise. It turns out that most mergers and acquisitions destroy real value. In the year 2000, for instance, AOL merged with Time Warner in a huge $350 billion deal. Meant to create an integrated new-media powerhouse, the merger went downhill almost immediately. A decade later, the unmerged companies are now worth just one-seventh of their premerger selves.[20] Yet investment firms Salomon Smith Barney and Morgan Stanley each collected $60 million in fees just the same.[21]

Then there are the hedge funds, which work to exploit volatility—and will actually work to produce it, if necessary—seeking to arbitrage any weakness they see. In essence, these fund managers attempt to find the most naive fiduciary institution to gouge, regardless of what the gouging will do to the beneficiaries of that pension fund or charitable cause. And they will continue to arbitrage merrily away, even if such actions help to bring the whole market to the edge of destruction, as they did in the 2008–2009 financial crisis. In late 2008, the SEC went so far as to ban short selling on some eight hundred financial products companies after claims were made that hedge funds and other market makers were targeting the firms (and others have claimed that naked short selling may have accelerated the declines of Bear Sterns and Lehman Brothers).[22]

And the final member of the expectations community is the financial press. Ultimately, the financial press wants a good story. So reporters will pump executives for details and quotes, eager to fill inches of column space. This can create a sinister compact—preferential access for positive coverage—in which the media serves as accessory to the executives, publicizing the party line to pump up or minimize expectations as the firm requires. But the relationship can have a dramatic downside for executives as well. Just as executives are able to exploit the financial media for their own ends, the media can turn on a company quickly and savagely, gleefully tearing down icons and highlighting stories of unmet expectations. Dashed hopes make excellent stories; they are full of angst and anguish—and sell lots of papers. Witness the feeding frenzies around former media darlings like Lehman's Dick Fuld (once one of *Barron's* Top 30 CEOs) and Hewlett-Packard's Mark Hurd (one of *Fortune*'s Power 25).[23]

To be a valued member of the expectations community, a CEO has to give guidance to analysts on things she can't actually predict—and then make the predictions come true; she must undertake transactions that provide the investment bankers with fees but return little to the firm; she must provide arbitrage opportunities for the hedge funds and offer stories for the financial press, all the while keeping shareholder value rising perpetually for institutional investors. Little of this produces anything good for the company, and most CEOs know it. That the community causes them to act without authenticity is unfortunate, but the allure of belonging to a community, even an unhealthy one, is strong indeed.

The modern CEO has been told in no uncertain terms that increasing shareholder value is her core purpose. But, other than herself and her executive team, those shareholders are faceless, nameless people represented by fiduciary institutions, like Fidelity and CalPERS, who can and will terminate the relationship for any reason, at any time, without warning or explanation.[24] Are these the people to whom the CEO really wants to dedicate her life? It means spending the majority of each day attempting to maximize the wealth of anonymous people with whom she has the shallowest of possible relationships. It is hardly deeply motivating. In fact, it is alienating.

So too is game playing with analysts. In the current structure, the CEO spends oodles of time trying to talk analysts' expectations into line with what the company can really do, instead of talking to customers in the real market. The task is painful, time-consuming, and difficult, made more so because it has to be accomplished without contravening Regulation Fair Disclosure (the SEC mandate that all publicly traded companies must disclose material information to all investors at the same time); every analyst, no matter how idiosyncratic his or her viewpoint, must be told the same things as everyone else. And, in the end, the task may be fruitless anyway. No matter how persuasive the CEO is with analysts, she always runs the risk that the market will run far ahead of reality anyway. Expectations swing wildly—more so than real returns.

The CEO's compensation package is chock-full of stock-based incentive compensation, so she has clear reasons to do all she can to increase the stock price. Yet she understands just as clearly that she can't do so forever—especially in the face of market overreactions. She has been set up to play a game she can't win, in concert with players she can't trust or doesn't really know. No wonder she games the game. She maximizes her own self-interest because it is a meaningful goal she can accomplish and because maximizing an anonymous shareholder's interests is both impossible over the long term and ultimately meaningless. In the midst of an unhealthy community, the CEO leads an inauthentic life, doing whatever it takes to feed the expectations beast—sacrificing healthy relationships with customers, employees, hometowns, and long-term investors along the way.

The CEO behaves, in other words, as Philip Condit, former CEO of Boeing, did. In 2001, in the interest of maximizing value for his multitude of anonymous owners, Condit essentially put the location of Boeing's headquarters out to tender. He announced that Boeing would leave its longtime headquarters in Seattle for whichever city could deliver the best package of incentives and credits. Chicago won, offering the biggest municipal bribe (oops, I meant "incentive"). Boeing forsook Seattle, its home for eighty-five years, for an offer from the highest bidder. But even that mercenary move wasn't enough for the expectations beast. Short-term shareholders kept pressuring Boeing for ever higher earnings increases. In its efforts to satisfy them, Boeing engaged in procurement corruption and industrial espionage, which resulted in huge fines, jail terms, and the forced resignation of Condit (and, in due course, of his successor as well).

Undoubtedly, there is no one reason for the fall of Boeing. But certainly a contributing factor was the replacement of a community of real, long-term investors with anonymous, short-term, shareholders, and a shift in the purpose of the firm from producing great products and great jobs to producing shareholder value. As a result of these changes, longtime Seattle jobs could be destroyed to create shareholder-value-friendly jobs in Chicago. Rules could be bent—or broken outright—to increase earnings for a community of transitory shareholders.

Boeing was an iconic, great American firm, a stalwart of the Pacific Northwest. That it fell prey to the siren call of shareholder value so dramatically, leading to corruption and espionage, is both heartbreaking and hard to fathom. So, too, is the pervasiveness of the flat-out fraud of options backdating and the dangerous expansion of *NINJA* (no-income, no-job, no-assets) mortgages, repackaged in elegant slices and sold to hopelessly naive investors. In each case, values and ethics fell by the wayside.

Why?

Bruce Springsteen explained the phenomenon in his 1973 classic "It's Hard to Be a Saint in the City":

> *The devil appeared like Jesus through the steam in the street*
> *Showin' me a hand I knew even the cops couldn't beat.*"[25]

The criminal behavior that drove both stock option backdating and NINJA mortgages can be understood through the nature of the communities in which executives now live; like the devil in Springsteen's city, these communities show their members' hands that the cops find hard to beat.

In Silicon Valley, it made good sense to backdate options because it helped the companies win the war for talent and to maximize shareholder value (or at least value for some shareholders). Companies wanted to be valued members of the Silicon Valley corporate community, and backdating options was what it took to be a player there. Similarly, it made sense for Wall Street bankers to slice, dice, and repackage mortgages, and to foist the new securities on investors who didn't understand them, because that was what it took to succeed in the Wall Street community—and being a valued member of that community was important, because, until late 2008, Wall Street was flying high.

Again, everyone wants to be part of a community, however unhealthy that community may be. So CEOs drink the Kool-Aid of shareholder value and dedicate themselves to the community of shareholder value maximizers. They become inauthentic as their jobs are stripped of the real meaning they once held. J&J harks back to an earlier, more authentic era when it touts its commitment to its customers, its employees, and the communities in which it operates. In contrast, when shareholder value moves to the front of the queue, the rest of the community suffers: CEOs will dupe customers to meet expectations; they will sack employees to meet expectations; and they will spoil the environment to meet expectations. These actions are not taken for the purpose of earning a satisfactory return on the money provided to the company by shareholders; they are taken to chase expectations that are entirely ethereal.

This is what it means to be inauthentic: it is to become someone you are not in order to satisfy those outside you—the members of your unhealthy community. In short order, the moral compass breaks down and immoral, illegal behavior runs rampant. But inauthentic behavior is not inevitable. If we refocus the CEOs on communities that are both healthy and meaningful, we have a hope of returning authenticity to the C-suite.

RESTORING HEALTH AND AUTHENTICITY

In 1978, Václav Havel wrote an essay called *The Power of the Powerless*, addressed to Lech Wałęsa and his comrades in the Gdansk shipyards in Poland.[26] In it, Havel explored how the Soviet Union was able to maintain control of its subjects at home and in the Warsaw Pact countries—including in Havel's own Czechoslovakia and Wałęsa's Poland (the Gdansk shipyards excepted). The essay, in support of Wałęsa's strike, was about the power of authenticity and the cost of its absence.

The Soviet Union, Havel argued, was able to maintain control by forcing its subjects to live a lie—in essence, to be inauthentic. Havel illustrated the nature of this lie through the story of a shopkeeper told to keep a sign emblazoned with "Workers of the World Unite" in his store window. The shopkeeper knew that the Soviet Union had long ceased to be about uniting the workers of the world and was now about a brutal ruling class subjugating its people. So he knew that to put the sign in the window would be to live a lie. But he complied because he was afraid of the consequences of insubordination. And in acquiescing to the sign, the shopkeeper publicly gave control to the authorities who had forced the lie on him.

In Havel's view, Wałęsa and the strikers were renouncing the lie and refusing to live within it. By organizing a labor strike against the rulers of the supposed workers' paradise, Wałęsa and his fellows were being authentic and also exposing the lack of authenticity of their Communist rulers. Havel predicted that such acts would bring down the Soviet Union—and history bears him out. The strikers prevailed and delivered a crucial blow to the Soviet empire, which crumbled within a decade.

By allowing an unhealthy community to surround our CEOs and senior executives, we are encouraging them to live an inauthentic life—like so many Soviet-era shopkeepers. This saps the moral authority of the business community and causes many talented young people to avoid it in order to retain their own authenticity. For that reason, for the future of business itself, it is imperative that we improve the health and authenticity of our business community and its leaders.

The straightforward answer is to simply tell CEOs to ignore the expectations market. And indeed, some argue that this is the right approach. Michael Jensen, for instance, paired with consultant Joe Fuller to pen *Just Say No to Wall Street: Putting a Stop to the Earnings Game.*[27] The Aspen Institute's Corporate Values Strategy Group has been working since 2003 on "promoting changes in corporate and investment practice, as well as in public policy, to support long-term orientation in business decision making and investing." In 2009, it issued *Overcoming Short-termism: A Call for a More Responsible Approach to Investment and Business Management*, a paper encouraging both investors and executives to think longer term.[28]

But admonishing CEOs (and investors) to ignore the expectations market is about as effective as admonishing frat boys to stop chasing girls. For CEOs, there is little support in resisting the pull of the expectations market and great rewards for staying attuned to it. Investors, analysts, and hedge funds are all creatures of the expectations market and they continue to reward firms that meet expectations and punish those that do not. Bartov,

Givoly, and Hayn demonstrated empirically that there are clear consequences to failing to meet or beat expectations.[29] What's more, accountants are waiting in the wings to force write-downs of real assets if the stock price falls. Missing expectations, a dropping stock-price, and real-asset write-downs can together create an unstoppable downward spiral. In the current environment, to simply ignore the expectations market is to court disaster.

The other fundamental problem with admonishing CEOs to ignore the expectations market is that it means asking them to be insubordinate. Incentive compensation systems are designed with a purpose: to encourage the person covered by the incentive plan to produce the outcomes targeted by the incentive structure. If a saleswoman is given an incentive structure with a substantial bonus for achieving a specified sales quota, and she makes no attempt to achieve the quota and earn the bonus, she is being insubordinate. The incentive was put in place to encourage the behavior desired. If the company wanted her to take long lunches rather than sell products, it would have created an incentive plan that set a quota for long lunches and a bonus for achieving that quota.

When a board gives its CEO stock-based incentive compensation, whether stock options, stock, or phantom stock, it is issuing an incentive to do one thing and one thing only: raise expectations from the current level to a higher level. If expectations are not raised from the current level, incentive compensation will not be earned. If the CEO doesn't attempt to raise expectations, he is showing no regard for the incentive structure that was put in place. He is being insubordinate. We can't expect CEOs en masse to be fundamentally insubordinate in order to follow our admonitions to ignore Wall Street.

Many, including Michael Jensen, argue that we shouldn't throw out stock-based incentive compensation entirely, but that we must instead fix its structure and use. If stock options are the problem, they argue, options should be replaced with deferred stock units set out over a much longer term. They go on to argue that we need to rein in the out-of-control compensation consultants and to develop more knowledge and discipline on the compensation committees that design stock-based incentive systems.[30] Indeed, compensation structures, compensation consultants, and compensation committees all present problems. But they are problematic because of the theory they employ, not in and of themselves: when an unsustainable game is being played, game structures are going to be awfully hard to manage, consultants are going push the boundaries of the rules, and committees are going to be confused. But that hardly implies that the structures, consultants, and committees are the root of the problem.

The fundamental problem with stock-based incentives is that they direct the recipient to try to raise expectations from the current expectation level. Though Jack Welch and Bill Gates showed that, if one is clever and determined, one can do that for a long time, it can't be done forever. So there will be bad behavior. There will be earnings guidance, earnings management, accounting fraud, and crazy bubbles. The focus will be on covert manipulation of results and expectations rather than on building for the future. These aren't random happenings; these are the direct consequences of the core theory.

The only way to restore the focus of the executive on the real market and on an authentic life is to eliminate the use of stock-based compensation as an incentive. This doesn't mean that executives shouldn't own shares. If an executive wants to buy stock as some sort of bonding with the shareholders or for whatever other reasons, that's just fine. However, executives should be prevented from selling any stock, for any reason, while serving in that capacity—and indeed for several years after leaving their posts.

While this may seem radical, let's remember, it worked very well for the majority of the history of modern business. As late as the early 1970s, stock-based compensation was rare and made up a minuscule fraction of the compensation for CEOs of S&P 500 firms. In 1970, CEOs earned an average of $850,000 (in constant dollars), a tidy sum at the time, and less than 1 percent of that was earned through stock-based compensation. By 2000, CEOs averaged $14 million in compensation, with 50 percent coming from stock options.[31] And recall that shareholders actually did better in the earlier period. Stock-based compensation is a very recent phenomenon, one associated with lower shareholder returns, bubbles and crashes, and huge corporate scandals.

Of course, CEOs may well balk at this prescription, because stock-based compensation has been instrumental in dramatically increasing their average compensation. It will take the concerted efforts of boards and investors to eliminate the scourge of stock-based incentive compensation. The only form of stock-based incentive compensation that should be used is stock-based compensation that vests after the recipient's retirement—preferably three or more years after retirement.

Stock-based compensation of this sort would discourage executives from driving a wedge between expectations and reality, then exploiting it at the expense of shareholders. It would also eliminate the popular practice of executives driving up expectations to a crescendo and then retiring to cash in stock-based compensation as expectations collapse on the head of their successors. Finally, it would enforce discipline on CEOs (and their boards), directing them to spend the necessary time and energy on selecting and preparing a successor. If a CEO focused on the real market, worked toward long-term profitability, and groomed the next CEO for success, three years after retirement she would receive a very big bonus—one that would be good for her, for the shareholders, and for the economy.

We also need to break executives of the guidance habit. As suggested in chapter 2, we can start by undoing the safe harbor provision of the Private Securities Litigation Reform Act, turning guidance back into a dangerous act. There is simply no societal value to earnings guidance. The market will know exactly what earnings are going to be at the end of the quarter, in just three or fewer months. Society is not better off to have an executive publicly guess at what that number is going to be. We need to turn executives from the useless, vapid task of managing expectations to the psychologically rewarding business of creating value.

Analysts will continue to estimate earnings and the media will continue to use consensus estimates as a benchmark against which real performance of a company is measured. Putting a stop to the conversation between companies, analysts, and the media is unlikely, so it is up to the CEO to change the nature of the conversation. The CEO should aim to establish the widest possible range of potential outcomes on the narrowest set of measures when speaking about the future of the company, so that the company has the freedom to make smart, long-term investment decisions that might otherwise cause it to miss a narrowly defined target in a specific quarter. Beyond that, as the CFO of one of America's largest and most successful companies recently told me, the company should "let the results speak for themselves, and let them speak over time."

USEFUL INCENTIVE COMPENSATION

If stock-based compensation doesn't work, what then is the nature of useful incentive compensation? Before diving into an answer, we must observe one important caveat: while we tend to assume that there is a causal link between incentive compensation and corporate performance, none has yet been found.[32] It seems to make logical sense that there would be a correlation, but there isn't. Companies with heavy monetary incentive compensation have not been shown to outperform companies without.

However, we do know that individuals are motivated by financial incentives. A classic study by sociologist Donald Roy demonstrated that even uneducated machine-shop workers would bend their work patterns into a metaphorical pretzel to optimize their daily compensation. On certain days, that meant working efficiently and effectively, but for only a few hours, while on other days, it meant working inefficiently and ineffectively for the full shift. Given the patterns and type of work available, the workers figured out how to game the system with one goal in mind: maximizing piecework-based daily pay.[33]

Roy's study provided a very important insight: monetary incentives result in extremes of behavior. The machine-shop workers pushed their piecework earnings to the maximum possible on the days they were assigned "gravy" jobs and the minimum possible without getting fired on days they were assigned "stinker" jobs. There were almost no outcomes between the extremes.

On one hand, monetary incentives can produce genuinely helpful results, as did the completion-time incentives offered to construction firms after the 1994 Northridge California earthquake. Roads and bridges were rebuilt in a fraction of the predicted time, using a 24/7 work model instead of the usual 9-to-5 clock-punching mode. But on the other hand, monetary incentives generated massive fraud when Sears decided to give its Auto Center employees compensation based on the average revenue per customer visit. Suddenly, its employees began to convince customers that lots of things needed fixing that actually didn't. The result: $400 million in overcharges to 30 million customers over the years from 1989 to 1999 and a tattered reputation for the retail icon.[34] Even the best of companies find it enormously challenging to design a monetary incentive system that is meaningfully balanced.

The other fundamental problem with monetary incentive compensation is that, if it works, it tends to focus the recipient on maximizing his own incentive compensation at the expense of other tasks. If the executive ignores the incentive compensation system and goes about his work as if it didn't exist, then the incentive payments were completely wasted; the executive did what he would have done regardless of the incentive. If, on the other hand, an executive is motivated by the incentive, he will attempt to maximize that incentive compensation, making decisions for personal benefit but not necessarily that of the company. In due course, colleagues and customers will figure out exactly where they stand in the pecking order: behind the personal profit-maximizing of the executive.

In this respect, the executive mirrors the firm. The firm attempts to maximize shareholder value and the executive attempts to maximize personal incentive compensation. In such a context, there is no incentive to maximize customer delight. Rather, customers simply impose a minimum constraint; as long as the company and its employees don't treat the customer too badly, they will stick around. This is a recipe for guaranteeing customers that are devoid of delight, ripe for poaching by competitors.

More useful incentives encourage the executive to become a valued member of a company community dedicated to delighting the customer. Such incentives include a mix of monetary and psychological compensation, both extrinsic and intrinsic motivation. To return to the NFL metaphor, the running back doesn't stretch another yard to try to make the first down because doing so will earn him a bonus check; he does it to help win, to excite the fans, and to be seen by his colleagues as working his hardest on the task. If he does stretch that extra yard, will the outcome be devoid of monetary reward? Not at all. If he does it consistently, the next contract he signs will be for more money. But that reward comes further down the line.

Net, we would do well to replace the pursuit of personal monetary goals with the pursuit of a broader set of goals, which includes delighting one's customers. Monetary incentives are not to be ignored by any means, but nonmonetary incentives—the feeling of pride in contributing to a company's goal, in offering the best product or service to customers—should compete closely. If a firm is more than simply a moneymaking machine, its executives are better able to see their role as being more than a personal moneymaking machine.

With respect to monetary incentives, one rule is crystal clear: they should be grounded entirely in the real market. They should provide motivations to produce real outcomes, not expectations market outcomes. The particular real measure will depend entirely on the industry and its particular context; it may be return on invested capital, market share, cash management, turnover/retention, project management, or another measure; regardless, it should ultimately encourage the provision of better value to the customer.

Shifting from expectations measures to real ones is possible for even the largest companies. Like many of its peers, Procter & Gamble once used total shareholder return (TSR) as a key measure in its compensation system. TSR was defined as the increase in share price plus dividends (as if reinvested in stock) over a three-year period. Under that system, P&G's TSR was benchmarked against that of a peer group; if P&G was in the upper half of the group, its executives received bonuses. In the early 2000s, P&G moved to a real-market system, creating something called *operating TSR*, which is a combination of three real operating performance measures— sales growth, profit margin improvement, and increase in capital efficiency. This is now the basis on which it compensates its executives, and it lets the share price take care of itself.

The usual argument against such real measures, as opposed to expectations-based stock measures, is that the former fail to reward executives for long-term value creation. The argument goes that, since the stock price incorporates all likely future cash flows attributable to current initiatives, a CEO who improves long-term cash flows would be rewarded for that properly with stock-based compensation and under-rewarded with real-market-based compensation. While this critique has merit, the problem is not a function of a reality-based compensation system, but rather of the lack of creativity in the design of compensation systems. To capture long-term value creation in a reality-based incentive compensation system, the reward can be structured as a royalty, an approach that works well in many industries today. When Herman Miller launched the Aeron chair, which became the most successful chair in the history of the planet, its designers, outsiders Bill Stumpf and Don Chadwick were granted royalty checks, rewards that have kept coming as the Aeron has kept selling and selling. As a result, every furniture designer in the world would like to design the next Aeron for Herman Miller. Similarly, musicians and actors get residuals; patent holders get licensing fees. These are all methodologies for capturing rewards from the creation of long-term value in the real market.

There really is no problem in creating sensible and productive incentives for long-term value creation without going anywhere near the expectations market. It is merely the desire to try and the insight to find a creative answer connected to the real market. With such creativity, we can create more authentic compensation systems and, ultimately, more authentic executives.

FOUR

REPAIRING GOVERNANCE

A "no" uttered from deepest conviction is better
and greater than a "yes" merely uttered to please,
or what is worse, to avoid trouble.

—Mahatma Gandhi

Baseball is the American pastime. As Annie Savoy, Susan Sarandon's baseball-obsessed character in *Bull Durham* tells us, even the great poet Walt Whitman was beguiled by it. Annie quotes Whitman: "I see great things in baseball. It's our game, the American game. It will repair our losses and be a blessing to us."

Indeed, for more than a hundred years, every year from April to October, baseball was a cornerstone of what it meant to be American, up there, famously, with Mom and apple pie. Kids played sandlot ball, dreamed of making it to the big leagues, and shared in the heroics of their favorite professional players, legends like Babe

Ruth, Joe DiMaggio, Ted Williams, Mickey Mantle, and Cal Ripken Jr. Baseball even informed American life, as the integration of Major League Baseball (MLB), beginning with Jackie Robinson in the 1940s, presaged the civil rights movement. Such was baseball's allure that, throughout much of the twentieth century, MLB was able to grow and expand across the continent, from sixteen teams to thirty by 1998.

But by the late 1990s, and certainly by the 2000s, something had changed. Americans grew less interested in their pastime. In 1980, when the Philadelphia Phillies played the Kansas City Royals in the World Series, an average of more than 40 million people watched on television.[1] By contrast, the 2010 series between the San Francisco Giants and the Texas Rangers drew an average of fewer than 15 million viewers.[2] The 2010 numbers weren't an anomaly. Ratings for baseball overall, and for the World Series in particular, have declined dramatically over the past thirty years. In fact, the average nationally broadcast regular-season NFL game now earns a higher television audience than do World Series games.[3] No wonder the NFL's current broadcasting agreement at $4 billion per year dwarfs baseball's agreement at $670 million a year over many more games.[4]

And it isn't just television; professional football has outperformed baseball on the financial dimension too. In the past decade, the total value of the NFL teams has risen from $11.6 billion to $33.3 billion: over $1 billion for each of the thirty-two teams. MLB has grown in value too, from $6.6 billion to $14.1 billion ($470 million on average per team), but its relative value has shrunk from 57 percent of the NFL to 42 percent in a mere decade.[5]

What's more, football has won the hearts and minds of Americans. When Americans are asked to name their favorite sport, 30 percent of them cite professional football, compared to 15 percent for baseball and 12 percent for college football.[6] On almost every dimension, football has overtaken baseball as America's game.

How can we explain the change? Some would make sense of baseball's relative decline by pointing to the dampening effect of MLB's labor unrest in the 1990s. Some would argue that MLB expanded too far, too fast. Still others would cite the fan disillusionment that followed revelations about baseball's steroids era. But these are merely symptoms of a larger systemic problem: governance is critical to organizational success, and it is on this dimension that the NFL truly outperforms MLB. At a governance level, the NFL has demonstrated continuity, purpose, and diligence, while MLB has demonstrated none of these.

Baseball has had seven different commissioners in the last fifty years. Most had either no previous experience in baseball management (Spike Eckert and Peter Ueberroth) or minimal experience (Bart Giamatti and Fay Vincent). The current commissioner came to the job in a circular and sinister way: in 1992, Bud Selig was the leader of a group of owners who forced the ouster of his predecessor, Fay Vincent. The same group then installed Selig as acting commissioner as they searched for a replacement. Almost incomprehensibly, a six-year search for a new commissioner netted no one, and Selig was eventually appointed on a permanent basis. A system that facilitates such a power grab is rarely indicative of good governance.

Arguably, MLB is run for the benefit of the owners and players, rather than for the fans. At the insistence of the players' union, there is no salary cap—just an ineffectual luxury tax—and little attempt at parity. The New York Yankees, who earn the most revenue, can afford to have a payroll that is 50 percent higher than any other team, making them the presumptive favorites to win the World Series every season. And while Selig demonstrated some willingness to take on the players—locking them out and cancelling the World Series in 1994—he has shown no such resolve to take on the owners. And no wonder: he has long been one of them. He retained ownership of his team, the Milwaukee Brewers, until 2005—despite the inherent conflict of interest in the league commissioner also being a team owner (even if the team was held in trust for most of his term).

When it comes to managing the game on the field, baseball takes a hands-off approach. There has been only one significant league-wide rule change since 1921: in 1968, it became clear that pitchers had gained a strong advantage over batters (that year, in 21 percent of all games, one of the two teams failed to score a single run and players hit for the lowest batting average in baseball history—a paltry .237), so the league responded by lowering the pitcher's mound by five inches, lessening the pitchers' advantage.[7] The addition of the *designated hitter*, a player who bats in place of the pitcher, was the second major rule change in the past ninety years; but tellingly, only the American League was willing to adopt it. The National League preferred to maintain one of the least fan-friendly aspects of baseball: the pitcher pathetically attempting to hit. Net, baseball saw two major rule changes over almost a century. In fact, for an entire decade between 1996 and 2006, there were no rule changes of any sort at all.[8]

In the NFL, by contrast, there has been stable leadership that has been elected in an open and forthright manner, and an ongoing commitment to the customer. There have been only three commissioners in fifty years: Pete Rozelle (a former team executive) from 1960–1989; Paul Tagliabue (longtime NFL outside counsel) from 1989–2006; and Roger Goodell (who started as league office intern) since 2006. Unlike the shady, behind-the-scenes process in baseball, the procedure for electing a commissioner of the NFL is thorough, careful, and inclusive. When Goodell was elected, he won the job over four other strong candidates, each of whom had been carefully selected by a Tagliabue-appointed committee (headed by two respected team owners: Dan Rooney and Jimmy Richardson). To get the job, which he did only on the fifth ballot, Goodell was required to gain a two-thirds majority of the thirty-two voting team owners.

From the time of Rozelle's term, the NFL commissioner's office has governed football with a laserlike focus on the fan experience. Every year, the NFL competition committee pores over the stats and film, and tweaks the rules in order to maintain a balance between offense and defense and to protect the players that the fans come to watch—especially the quarterbacks and wide receivers. Rarely a year goes by without a significant rule tweak, visible to the fans and put in place to enhance their experience. The commissioner's office also periodically battles to preserve the salary cap and the free-agency rules, fighting the union and rogue owners to keep them from undermining the parity that has produced twelve different winners over the past twenty Super Bowls.[9]

The NFL takes governance, from the election of its officers to the continued evolution of its rules, very seriously. Baseball, on the other hand, has a governance structure that is ineffectual at best. MLB is geared toward maintaining the status quo and delivering value to owners, while the NFL governance is forward looking and fan-centric—which just so happens to deliver plenty of value to its owners. This dichotomy helps explain how and why football has so dramatically outpaced baseball over the past thirty years.

THE NATURE OF BOARDS

Governance structures look considerably different in business than they do in the NFL, and rightly so. Contexts differ, and so should governance structures. But there is much to be learned from the twin examples of MLB and the NFL, not least the dramatic effects on long-term financial performance of thoughtful oversight, careful succession planning, and genuine customer-centricity. The approach a company takes to governance—the theories it holds and the structures it builds—can create or destroy real value.

For public companies, boards have a particularly tricky task. In many respects, boards lie right at the intersection between the expectations market and the real market. From that position, over time, boards have come to govern operations in the real market to the benefit of actors in the expectations market. How? Boards attempt to ensure that employees in the real market show proper accountability for their decisions and the operations of the firm; they also attempt to ensure that shareholders in the expectations market have visibility into operations in the real market. In particular, the board's job is to protect shareholders, ensuring that executives are engaged in maximizing the return to the shareholders rather than to the executives themselves.

By and large, it is the independent directors who have been tasked with being the voice and protector of outside shareholders. Most boards are made up of independent, outside directors (individuals who have no connection to the company other than through their board seat) and a few inside directors (executive-owners, like the CEO). Within this structure, the role of shareholder white knight falls to the independent directors because inside directors are considered ill-equipped to perform it, especially to the extent that the inside directors have meaningful stock-based compensation. As actors in both the real and expectations markets, inside directors have a powerful incentive to focus on raising expectations, whether or not doing so is in service of the company's long-term, real-market performance. An inside director may attempt to show self-control and not act in accordance with this incentive, but it is a Herculean task. Therefore, inside directors are not at all well positioned to protect the interests of the outside shareholders, so the burden falls on independent directors, who, unfortunately, aren't well positioned to do it either.

THE PROBLEM WITH DIRECTORS

A board of directors is asked to span a wide (and widening) gulf, resolving the tension between two very different markets with very different actors. On the one hand, boards are intended to act on behalf of outside shareholders, who want the greatest possible return for their investment in the expectations market. On the other hand, the board must deal closely with executives, who work in the real market yet are tied by incentives to the expectations market and motivated to maximize their own returns, even at the expense of shareholders. And those executives are in fact in an ideal position to exploit outside shareholders; with deep insider knowledge, they know much better than any outsider could when to buy or sell the company's stock based on the greatest possible differential between expectations and reality. So, ultimately, the job of directors is to ensure that insiders do not use their preferential access to information to exploit outside shareholders. Unfortunately, it is a job directors can't perform effectively, owing to problems with capabilities, incentives, and selection.

Many jobs are difficult but can be accomplished by dedicated people with the right set of skills and capabilities.

One problem with the role we have given to outside directors is that no matter how dedicated the individuals involved, they will be largely incapable of achieving what we have asked of them. Independent directors can't know as much as management does about the operations of the firm. Their very independence puts them at a distinct information disadvantage relative to the inside directors. Executive management is in a position to provide independent directors with whatever information it sees fit and has the capacity to restrict access to information it doesn't want independent directors to see. No matter how smart and diligent the independent directors, they will never match the knowledge of executives, who, by definition, spend much more time engaged on the business than directors do. The best an independent director can do is to bring to bear broad expertise and insight from other markets that management can utilize if it so desires. But that isn't the task we set out for them; we don't ask them to make use of those capabilities. We ask them to be all-knowing, even when that is impossible.

Many assume that the knowledge deficit can be overcome through the hiring of professionals, principally auditors, by the independent committee of the board. Again, this simply is not the case. In the end, the important audit decisions come down to judgment, and management is always in a better position to argue its case than the auditors are to argue theirs. WorldCom provides an excellent object lesson on this. Its auditors did not discern that management had classified $3.8 billion in expenses as assets in order to inflate earnings.[10] Because the "assets" in question were various sorts of complicated switching gear in the WorldCom network, management was able to convince the auditors that this equipment would be used as an asset for years to come when, in fact, it was equipment that had been purchased and installed to serve a single client, and had no obvious further use. The equipment should properly have been expensed against the profitability of the client contract, not capitalized and put on the books of WorldCom as an asset. The insiders knew this, yet were able to use the information asymmetry to convince the outsiders otherwise. Increased scrutiny and regulatory changes in the wake of the recent scandals has emboldened auditors, but none of the changes will help them overcome this inherent knowledge deficit.

The capabilities challenge is stiff. When the outside shareholders of Enron needed the independent directors to stop illegal accounting, blatant self-dealing, and stunning market exploitation by CEO Jeff Skilling and CFO Andrew Fastow, the independent directors were incapable of doing so. When the outside shareholders of Qwest Communications needed the independent directors to alert them to the fact that insiders were exploiting the mismatch between the expectations market and the real market (unloading $2 billion in stock before the bottom dropped out of the share price), the directors were unable to do so. Independent directors—even bright, capable, and dedicated ones—simply don't have a chance against executives committed to their own self-interest.[11]

But the capability issue is only part of the problem. Not only do independent directors lack the *capability* to effectively serve the interests of outside shareholders, they also lack the *incentive* to do so. We know that people respond to incentives. And recall that agency theory tells us that people have self-interested motivations that cause them to maximize their own welfare instead of the welfare of the organization for which they work. So, the argument goes, executives (the agents) will maximize their own rewards at the expense of shareholders (the principals) unless given incentives to do otherwise. The theory suggests that we can deal with the principal-agent problem by having the board of directors discipline the agents and incent them effectively. But do boards not have exactly the same principal-agent problem? After all, the members of the board of directors are not principals either. They are agents too—hired and paid for by the shareholders—and, as agents, directors have every bit as much interest in maximizing their own welfare as do executives.

It raises the question: why would we imagine that the directorial agents would act any differently than the executive agents? After all, directors and executives are drawn largely from the same pool: current and former senior executives are highly sought as directors. Yet we choose to apply agency theory to executives and not to directors. We assume that executives will maximize their self-interest, but that directors will not. This is a failure of logic. Either the motivational schism between principals and agents is real and is a problem, or it's not. If it is not a problem, then we don't need directors to keep managers in line. But if it is a problem, then directors will be susceptible to the same incentive issues as executives, and having a board of directors won't do a company a bit of good.

Finally, in addition to problems of capabilities and incentives, boards of directors suffer from a profound selection problem that further prevents them from protecting outside shareholders effectively. Put simply, good governance is something companies tend to have when they don't need it and lack when they do.

At some companies, shareholders have little need for protection. These are the companies, like P&G and J&J, who put customers first, focus on the long term, and grow value consistently over time. They have nothing to hide from their shareholders, so have no reason not to have great, thoughtful directors; open communication between executives and the board; and full disclosure to directors. Their directors are therefore in the best possible position to keep tabs on wayward executives and to clamp down on them. But since such companies had nothing to hide in the first place, their directors rarely need to discipline the executives; the culture of the company already provides that discipline. Ultimately, while these companies have directors and board relationships that could overcome agency problems, there aren't agency problems to overcome.

Executives of companies with something to hide, on the other hand, will look for weak directors and will seek to obscure the truth. In these companies, executives don't want to enlighten directors or disclose the truth to them. They hide information, obscure facts, and do all they can to keep the directors ignorant of the company's real activities. At Enron and Qwest, for example, directors weren't up to the task of protecting shareholders precisely because they were at a company that so desperately needed them to be up to it. Executives made sure that directors weren't up to the task out of pure self-interest.

So the great irony is that where stellar performance by independent directors is most needed, it is least likely to happen and where great performance is least needed, it is most likely to happen. Essentially, board governance works like a driver's education course. Careful, dutiful new drivers take driver's education courses. Impulsive, bad new drivers don't, and so never improve. This is what economists call an adverse selection bias. Circumstances cause exactly the wrong drivers to select the option of taking a driver's education course. If we accept that boards exist to protect shareholders, then exactly the wrong companies have great, functioning boards.

MOTIVATIONS FOR JOINING A BOARD

Selection bias is a big issue for boards. People choose to become directors—they aren't forced to show up at the table—and they must have some reason, some motivation, for doing so. Unfortunately, most reasons to join a board are problematic from a governance point of view. In fact, there is a set of five such plausible motivations to join a board, each of which is unhelpful to the shareholders and to the company. From most to least concerning, they are:

- Personal or company favors

- Attractive compensation

- Personal prestige

- Social enjoyment

- Personal growth

Personal or Company Favors

One might join a board in order to attain favors for either one's company or for oneself. Though it might seem far-fetched, not too long ago it was common practice for a CEO to sit on the board of his company's biggest lender. The CEO would serve as director for his lead bank in part to ensure that his company wouldn't get cut off in a future credit crunch. More recently, as disclosure rules have made such arrangements less common, the practice has taken a more personal turn. Now, board membership can lead to consulting contracts or other nonmonetary benefits, such as prime seats to sporting or cultural events, for directors. While access to such small-time swag may not be a big piece of the motivation puzzle, it is an unalloyed negative for the company and its outside shareholders; directors motivated by personal or company considerations have incentive to trade votes in exchange for the desired favors, approving actions that enrich executives and other insiders at the expense of shareholders. Such directors are de facto bad for shareholders and bad for the company.

Attractive Compensation

Some directors join a board for the financial remuneration; that is, they view board membership as an attractive way to make money relative to other opportunities.

However, if this is the motivation for joining the board, the director will be inclined to act in whatever way is necessary to maintain a place on the board, since removal on the grounds of noncooperation would eliminate the compensation. Some companies attempt to make their boards more appealing by including significant stock-based compensation in the directors' pay package. But in this case, the compensation structure converts the individual from independent director into the moral equivalent of an executive-owner, with all the attendant problems and the selfsame incentive to focus on raising expectations instead of on real results. If compensation is the key motivator for an individual to join a board as an independent director, it is a bad thing for corporate governance.

Personal Prestige

Another potential motivation for joining a board is the status that accrues to a director of a publicly traded company. Indeed, directors are showered with positive attention. However, as with compensation, if this is the motivation for joining the board, the director will be inclined to act in whatever way is necessary to maintain a place on the board, in this case because removal from the board would diminish rather than add personal prestige. So net, the motivator of personal prestige is also an unhelpful thing for good governance.

Social Enjoyment

Yet another potential motivator is to become a valued member of an enjoyable and stimulating social community—the board in question. Given the earlier discussion of the drivers of happiness, it would be unsurprising if an individual were to seek to become a respected member of the community represented by a given board, especially if she respected that community and it was respected by the world at large. However, if community is the primary motivator for joining a board, the director in question will be inclined to strictly obey the cultural norms of the board in order to earn and maintain the respect of her fellow board members. This motivation is yet another incentive to not rock the boat.

The exact nature of the outcomes from this motivation depends on the dominant culture of the board. But whether the dominant culture favors executives over outside shareholders or protects outside shareholders from exploitation by management, the community-motivated director will simply acquiesce to the rest of the board. Thus, if the culture is bad, this independent director will not be motivated to improve it and if the culture is good, this independent director will be superfluous. So again, this is not a motivation that ends up increasing good governance.

Personal Growth

Many directors cite growth opportunities as their reason for joining a board. By that, they generally mean that they want to learn about a particular industry or about governance in general. This is a pretty benign motive compared with the reasons above. However, a director motivated by personal growth is unlikely to possess the knowledge and skills to provide meaningful governance protection for the outside shareholders, especially if doing so gets in the way of personal learning. Hence personal growth is another unhelpful motivation for serving as an independent director.

These five reasons comprise, I believe, the dominant reasons individuals join the boards of publicly traded companies as independent directors. And none of them make it likely that an individual will take a stand against executive management or fellow directors, even to stop them from doing something that would hurt the shareholders and the company long-term. Of course, things may turn out to be just fine. If executive management wants to do things that are in the best interests of the shareholders and company, directors motivated by some combination of these five factors will happily go along with the proposed direction. But in that case, the concurrence is of limited utility: the action would have happened anyway.

There is only one motivation for joining a board as an independent director that is actually good for the company long-term and good for the outside shareholders: *public service*.

Public Service

In this best-case scenario, independent directors are motivated by a desire to provide an important service to the public at large; for directors, that service is the safeguarding of an essential foundation of democratic capitalism—the belief that individuals can provide their capital to a company and have it treated with fairness and respect. Operating under this motivation, the director wouldn't demand that shareholder returns be maximized but, rather, he or she would work with executives to ensure that the company is sound and that a fair return on investment is earned. Such a director would seek to provide insight and guidance to the company and would be inclined to stand up for customers, employees, the community, and shareholders, regardless of the reaction of the rest of the board.

It is not clear that public-service-motivated directors are plentiful. Governance as public service is a hard job, one that requires deep knowledge and expertise, coupled with a willingness to accept a high opportunity cost and the likelihood of being consistently at odds with the immediate board community, all for the benefit of others. This is hardly an inherently attractive proposition. Plus, seeing independent directorship as public service goes against the grain of public opinion. If anything, the public sees directors as highly paid fat cats who smoke cigars, drink martinis, and line their own pockets with indulgent pay packages. So, even if individuals were willing to take on the task of being an independent director for public service reasons, it is unlikely, at least in the current environment, that their motivations would be seen in that light by others.

Yet the goal must be to have directors who have both the capabilities and the incentives to serve the shareholders. Under the current structure, adverse selection means the wrong people end up in the wrong jobs, and motivations drive the wrong kind of director behavior. Instead, we must reshape the meaning of board membership and redefine it as highly valued public service. To do so, it is important to reinforce the notion that good governance is essential not just to the protection of shareholders but to the functioning of our entire economy and our shared prosperity.

GOVERNANCE AND TRUST

In *Trust: The Social Virtues and the Creation of Prosperity*, Francis Fukuyama highlights a critically important aspect of governance: the generation of trust.[12] Fukuyama makes the central point that the prosperity of entire nations is a function of the broad institutionalization of trust in their economies. Economies like Nigeria, in which you can only trust your immediate family, have the lowest prosperity. Economies, such as Russia, in which you can trust the broad, extended family or clan, are more prosperous. In economies like Thailand, relatively established stock markets and commercial legal institutions engender trust outside the family, and these countries are the next most prosperous. Finally, economies in which there are robust legal institutions, an independent judiciary, advanced contract law, and well-regulated capital markets (for example, the major highly developed countries) are the most prosperous.

The most prosperous countries have become that way because capital formation can take place at a broad level. Individuals can trust their capital to people they don't even know because institutions such as securities commissions and commercial courts provide protection and recourse for individual investors and their capital. Where trust is low, capital cannot be gathered and deployed, and poverty is the result.

Fukuyama wasn't dealing directly with corporate governance (in fact, he was writing before the recent wave of governance scandals). But his work holds a powerful message: weak governance undermines trust, and anytime trust is undermined, prosperity suffers fundamentally. The institutions that underpin trust in our economy are essential to our standard of living. They are the difference between prosperity and poverty.

FIXING CORPORATE GOVERNANCE

If, because of capability and incentive problems, boards are unlikely to be useful just when they are most needed, the trust necessary for a prosperous economy will be eroded. Insurance policies that are in force all the time, except when something goes wrong, don't build trust. But if we can reframe the discussion and make it clear that to serve as a director is to protect the institutions that underpin our mutual trust and prosperity, being a director will be a noble calling. The fix won't be at all easy; it will require directors to behave differently and for the public to see directors in a different light, so that the public and directors become two sides that can reinforce one another.

To begin, the job description for directors needs to change. Like the folks who run the NFL, boards should be focused on governing with continuity, purpose, and diligence, not on delivering supernormal returns to shareholders. The problems with asking people to work hard to protect nameless, transient investors have been discussed at length. But so too have the positive effects of concentrating the firm on building meaningful relationships with customers. If directors were to frame their role as public service—protecting the institutions of business by auditing the operations of the firm, keeping management fixed on customers and on long-term, real-market goals—we would all be better off. In this case, boards would be seen as advisers and wise counselors, independent experts from whom management could seek guidance and insight on strategic choices. At board meetings, rather than looking to sell bulletproof ideas, executives would be able to improve their ideas through thoughtful discussion. Executive-board interactions would become far more productive, and actual value could be created.

Spend any length of time with directors of public companies under the current construct and you're likely to hear a legion of complaints:

"It is getting so hard."

"The liability is getting greater."

"With Sarbanes-Oxley, the meetings are getting longer and longer."

The problem with these complaints is that they accept a version of board directorship that is dictated by others. When directors complain that Sarbanes-Oxley and liability concerns are turning the board meeting into a long, bureaucratic, check-the-boxes exercise, they are blaming external pressures for an unpleasant experience. But these board members have a choice. They can choose to accept a check-the-box meeting, or they can rise above it and focus on doing their important public-service job: helping their company to perform well.

Whether about the nature of board work or about the level of associated fees, complaints such as those listed above diminish directors in the eyes of the public. If we want to reframe the role of directors, we need to attract more public-service-minded people to the job. And to do this effectively, public perception of what it means to be a director must shift. When current directors choose to complain about fees and regulations, the public sees them as greedy whiners who don't take pride in doing their job or as double-dealers who find regulations confining. What public-service-minded individual would want to join such a club?

Changing the way that boards frame their role, including stopping the complaints about fees and Sarbanes-Oxley, won't fix the inherent problems in corporate governance overnight. But it will start it moving in the right direction. Admitting that there are fundamental, structural challenges to good governance, rather than assuming away the principal-agent problem in respect to boards, is likely to help as well. It is hard to solve a problem if most argue it doesn't exist.

It will take time to shift the motivation of directors away from some combination of favors, compensation, prestige, social interaction, and personal growth to public service. In fact, it is possible that the job is too big and the point too esoteric; it may be that the majority of directors will never see it as their job to keep the focus on prospering in the real market—rather than manipulating the expectations market—in the service of democratic capitalism. But perhaps we can convert a smaller and more important subset of directors: board chairs. Board chairs are critically important, because they set the tone for the entire board. If board chairs are motivated by public service, many other board members will be drawn along with them in the right direction.

To make the shift to a public-service framework, board chairs need to be much more like judges. On the whole, judges are paid less than they could be paid as lawyers and face a largely thankless task that offers more hardship than exhilaration. But they do it because, in the legal profession, there is a strong sense that to become a judge is the highest form of public service—one that allows them to apply their wisdom and judgment to ensure that the judicial institution serves its country well. By and large—at least at the higher levels—judges take the bench out of a desire to serve the public, and the public recognizes this fact. If we could begin to see board chairs as we see judges, and if they could increasingly act in the public interest as judges do, even when it means taking unpleasant actions, we would improve the quality of governance of our publicly traded companies.

FIVE

THE INSANITY OF 2&20

I am a speculator. It accelerates the trend.
It gets you closer to the truth faster.

—James Simons

For most of human history, the power has belonged to
those who own the means of production. The owners of
the fiefdom, the estate, or the factory had the ability to
set the terms and conditions that governed all those
who toiled for them. No matter how harsh the conditions, how low the pay, or how demeaning the work,
owners could find someone willing to do it, and thus
commanded the balance of power. Yet by the end of the
twentieth century, the power had shifted so dramatically for a particular class of employees—corporate
executives—that we devised agency theory, stock-based
incentive compensation, and board governance to

prevent the owners (now called *shareholders*) from being exploited by these newly emboldened executives.

How did the balance of power shift so decisively? Trade unions can claim a small percentage of the credit; they got the ball rolling in America after the passage of the National Labor Relations Act in 1935, using collective bargaining to achieve higher wages and healthier conditions. But the most important cause was the shift from active owner-managers to professional managers. As the last century wore on, owners increasingly and willingly handed control of the means of production to CEOs and senior executives. As this shift took place, executives discovered that they had the broad ability to divert the resources of the firm into their own pockets, making themselves exceedingly rich. And they weren't alone: the last quarter of the twentieth century also saw a dramatic shift in the fortunes of professional athletes, who became very wealthy indeed, and a change in the way that creative artists, like filmmakers, were compensated for their work. In business, sports, and the film industry alike, workers have found a way to extract a greater and greater share of the wealth generated from their efforts.

TALENT GAINS THE UPPER HAND

As detailed in chapter 2, executives earned enormously greater incomes toward the end of the twentieth century, as the age of shareholder capitalism advanced—eight times more per dollar of profit generated for their share-holders on average for CEOs in 2000 versus 1980. But this was part of a wider trend. Like CEOs, professional athletes earned good but not huge incomes prior to the 1970s. Mickey Mantle, the New York Yankees legend, for instance, earned about $100,000 per season in the late 1960s.[1] The average baseball player salary at the time? Under $25,000.[2] Adjusted for inflation, that's about $600,000 a year for Mantle and $150,000 for the average player. Today, the Yankees' Alex Rodriguez earns $33 million a season and the average major leaguer gets almost $3.3 million.[3]

In Mantle's day, players weren't able to extract a high percentage of the money earned from their efforts because the owners kept the revenue for themselves. In each sport, a single league represented the pinnacle of achievement, offered the most desirable jobs, and so dictated the terms of employment. Run by a close-knit coalition of team owners, these leagues held all of the power—they had the stadiums, the money, the fans—whereas the athletes, no matter how talented, were ultimately disposable. Another talented youngster would take any given player's place in an instant. So, for the most part, athletes lived in inden-tured servitude to the club that "owned" them, whether that was in the NFL, MLB, or NBA.

Every so often, rival leagues formed as a challenge to the monopolies, like the American Football League in

1960, the American Basketball Association in 1967, or the World Hockey Association (WHA) in 1972. These new leagues provided players with an alternative venue in which to peddle their wares and in doing so, handed them bargaining power in the original league. The upstart leagues would also offer higher salaries and more perks to lure players away from the incumbents. For instance, star college quarterback Joe Namath was drafted on the same day by the St. Louis Cardinals of the NFL and the New York Jets of the nascent AFL. Namath chose to sign with the Jets for a then-record salary of $427,000.[4] The Winnipeg Jets of the WHA were able to lure Bobby Hull away from the NHL's Chicago Blackhawks in a record-setting, ten-year, $2.7 million deal.[5] These deals gave the new leagues credibility and put upward pressure on the salaries in the original leagues.

In due course, owners in the senior leagues figured this out and saw just how unattractive the economics of competing for talent were. So, they bought out and absorbed the rival leagues. Competition for talent declined and owner-friendly equilibrium returned. In each case, after the league mergers, the players returned to a largely powerless state in which there was only one legitimate buyer for their services, and the owners breathed a collective sigh of relief.

But all of that would soon change. The cracks first began to show in baseball, and soon spread. It started in

1970, when veteran outfielder Curt Flood, angry about being traded from the championship-contending St. Louis Cardinals to the cellar-dwelling Philadelphia Phillies, refused to report to his new team and launched a court battle to overturn the reserve clause in the standard baseball contract.

The *reserve clause* allowed a team to retain the rights to a player for a full year after a contract had expired. In essence, a player at the end of his contract had two options: sign a new contract with his current team or hold out, refusing to play (and receiving no pay), in hopes that the club might release or trade him. If he were released, which was frankly unlikely unless he was no longer a useful player, he might entertain new contract offers from other teams on the open market. If he were traded, the choice of his new team was entirely up to his owners. Once traded, the player could negotiate a contract with the new team but could not sign with anyone else. And because the reserve clause showed up in contract after contract (and the owners were steadfast in their collective insistence on it), for all intents and purposes players were bound to their original team until such time as the team no longer wanted them.

Flood argued that baseball's reserve clause violated federal antitrust laws and was akin to slavery. Flood's case went all the way to the U.S. Supreme Court, with MLB fighting it tooth and nail on behalf of the owners.

In the end, Flood lost the case. He had missed the entire 1970 season and played the last few lackluster games of his career the following year. But Flood's failed attempt had set the wheels in motion, opening up the possibility for other players, and the union and agents that represented them, to take on the reserve clause in other ways.

The reserve clause had a powerful, punitive mechanism. A player would need to work a full season without pay in order to leave a team on his own terms; it was a very high hurdle, regardless of the potential reward at the end of that year. Thus, players simply chose to accept their fate. That is, until Los Angeles Dodgers star pitcher Andy Messersmith became so disenchanted with his team and his contract that he did indeed pitch the entire 1975 season without a contract in order to challenge the reserve clause after season's end. He played out the season and filed a grievance, along with Montreal Expos pitcher Dave McNally, who was injured during the season as he tried to play out his reserve year. At the end of the year, Messersmith and McNally, supported by the player's union president Marvin Miller, met league representatives in arbitration to settle the dispute.

The arbitrator assigned to the case decided in favor of the players, famously declaring them *free agents*—and in a flash, the world changed for professional sports. Once released, the genie of free agency could never be put back in the bottle. Each league scrambled to negotiate limits to total free agency with its unions, but ultimately players had gained the upper hand. Players were now able to sell themselves to the highest bidder, typically after a certain number of years of service to their initial owner, changing what it meant economically to be a professional athlete.

Instead of earning a comfortable living, the best players began to get massively rich, with eight-figure annual salaries and nine-figure long-term contracts becoming the norm. In 2007, Alex Rodriguez signed a ten-year contract with the New York Yankees worth $275 million.[6] In 2010, the New England Patriots' Tom Brady signed a new four-year deal worth $78 million.[7] Each is the highest-paid player in his sport (for now). Free agency has given talent much more control than it ever had before.

TALENT OVERTAKES CAPITAL AT THE BOX OFFICE

Athletes were soon joined in their good fortune by creative artists in the film industry. Just a few years after the introduction of the free agent in baseball, super-agent Tom Pollock walked into the offices of Paramount Pictures to negotiate a deal for his client's next movie. His client was director, screenwriter, and special-effects genius George Lucas, flush with the success of the 1977

Star Wars, one of the most influential and successful films of all time. Earning over $300 million in its original release, *Star Wars* is still the second-highest-grossing film of all time when box office revenues are adjusted for inflation.[8] The next project on Lucas' docket was called *Raiders of the Lost Ark*.

In Hollywood, since the days of legendary studio heads Louis B. Mayer and Jack Warner, studios garnered the majority of profits for a film. In fact, in the early days, artists were treated much like pre-free-agency athletes—they signed long-term contracts with a single studio and made whatever movies that studio demanded of them.[9] That structure, known as the *studio system*, had broken down by the 1960s, as actors, in particular, began to recognize the power that their visibility and popularity with the audience gave them.

By the 1970s, typically, a screenwriter, director, or actor was paid a flat salary in advance of a film's release, signing individual contracts per film and no longer tied to any one studio. Though some of the most successful artists were able to negotiate percentage-of-the-profit deals, beginning with Jimmy Stewart for the movie *Winchester '73* in 1950, this approach was still rare. Lucas and Pollock wanted to change all that. The deal they proposed to Paramount was stunning. It called for Lucas to receive 50 percent of gross operating profits (that is, profits before studio overhead and marketing and distribution costs) for

Raiders of the Lost Ark for no financial investment on his part whatsoever. Playing five studios against one another for the rights to the film, Pollock managed to convince Paramount president Michael Eisner and chairman Barry Diller to agree to his terms. In doing so, he helped Lucas jump-start his journey toward multibillionaire status and changed the game for the rest of Hollywood. With the *Raiders* deal, Hollywood economics turned decisively in favor of talent (employees) over capital (studio owners), and it wasn't long until the price for an A-list leading actor hit $25 million per picture. In 2010, it went yet further: Leonardo DiCaprio elected to forgo a traditional salary for his film *Inception*, taking a percentage of the gross instead. The deal is said to have earned DiCaprio a cool $50 million.[10]

By the 1970s, across fields, talent was using whatever mechanisms it had to gain control over owners, and individuals were able extract greater and greater proportions of the fruits of their labor. This in itself isn't a bad thing. Since talent drives the creation of new ideas and the actual productivity of an economy, it should be rewarded for its efforts. But the extent of the shift in power was remarkable, and it created an environment in which the extraction of value for personal gain—at the expense of owners and other stakeholders—was the norm. This new normal enabled the emergence of the most effective value-extraction machine yet: the 2&20 formula.

TALENT OVER CAPITAL IN THE
FINANCIAL MARKETS

Until the final quarter of the twentieth century, the business of investment management was relatively stable, straightforward, and boring. Professionals managed the assets of capital holders under fairly simple arrangements. Stockbrokers got paid by the transaction, receiving a standard commission on the trades they performed for their clients. Their more upscale brethren, the investment managers, charged a fixed fee—typically 1 percent but sometimes as much as 2 percent—of assets under management. There was terrific leverage in such a model: One percent doesn't sound like much, but consider an investment firm with $10 billion in assets under management. That's $100 million in fees per year—enough to pay for a lot of support staff, plus some swanky offices, and still have plenty in the till for the principals themselves. So, investment management talent made a perfectly good living under these arrangements (and a great living if the pools of capital were sufficiently large). But the real winners in this structure were the investors—they paid a modest fixed fee for the expertise of investment managers and in return reaped almost all of the upside of the investments, which could be enormous.

In 1978, as Lucas was extracting his reward from Paramount, investment manager Theodore Forstmann decided that investors were getting too easy a ride. He felt that his track record of earning attractive returns for his clients justified charging a higher fee under a brand-new structure. He formed Forstmann Little and Company and announced that it would keep a 2 percent fee on assets under management, as many firms did, but that it would also charge investors 20 percent of the upside generated on their capital. This 20 percent surcharge became known as the *carried interest* or simply *the carry*.

Forstmann's new structure was highly consistent with the emerging thinking of the day. Michael Jensen and William Meckling had just introduced the concept of aligned interests to the world. While they focused on creating alignment between public company shareholders and the executives who managed their firm, it was an easy mental step to analogize to investors and the professionals who managed their investments. Surely their interests needed to be aligned too! Forstmann's formula was intended to do just that: if Forstmann did well for the investors, he did well for himself. The structure therefore had profound moral authority.

The 2&20 formula, as it soon became called, spread far and wide to all forms of nonpublic investments, including leveraged buyouts (LBOs), venture capital (VC), and hedge funds. The LBO market was really emerging at around the same time—in fact, Forstmann Little and Company was a pioneer in that particular form of investment. It bought companies, turned them around, and sold them for a profit, taking 2 percent of the value of the firm per year and 20 percent of the profit it earned for the limited partners (that is, investors) of its fund. As venture capital grew from a tiny industry to a giant investment category through the 1980s and 1990s, 2&20 became the exclusive formula for venture funds too. The hedge fund industry, which had been around since 1949 but grew explosively from a $100 billion industry in the mid-1990s to a trillion dollar industry only a decade later, enthusiastically adopted 2&20 as well.

All these forms of investment came to be called *private equity*. All were vehicles that were not sold to the public at large and that therefore didn't require a disclosure prospectus approved by regulators. Thus, the principals of the investment firms behind these vehicles didn't even have to argue for the formula. It was simply and clearly the standard, one that was seen to be entirely virtuous. The 2&20 model aligned the interests of investment firms with their clients, and who was to argue with that? So pervasive was the 2&20 approach that any firm that didn't use this structure suffered in the eyes of investors and the media; if a firm proposed to charge you less than 2&20, the theory went, that firm was probably no good— and investors should stay away from it. Better to give away a 2 percent flat fee and 20 percent of a huge upside surge to a great investment firm than to give considerably less to a mediocre firm that would generate weak returns. In the public's view, all of the real players in the market charged 2&20.[11]

Forstmann's innovation gained rapid acceptance because it aligned so well with the prevailing theories of the day and due to its own elegant logical consistency. Soon, an unimagined magnitude of riches poured into the pockets of private equity investment managers. It is doubtful that Forstmann had any idea how many men and women would get monumentally rich on his innovative formula; had he known, he might have charged them a 2&20 licensing fee for using his formula!

The level of wealth creation driven by 2&20 has been nothing short of awe-inspiring. We tend to believe that entrepreneurship is the way to get superrich in America, whether in technology, like Bill Gates; oil, like John D. Rockefeller; retailing, like Sam Walton; or media, like William Randolph Hearst. And that might have been the case at one time, but not anymore. The *Forbes* 400 list identifies and ranks the richest Americans. Within thirty years of Forstmann's creation, it was clear that the best way to achieve a place on the list was to invest other people's money and get paid on the basis of the 2&20 formula. Of the richest four hundred Americans on the 2010 list, fifty got there thanks to 2&20, versus forty for technology, thirty-nine for media, thirty-eight for oil and gas, and twenty-eight for retailing.[12]

Flat out, 2&20 is the greatest wealth producer of our lifetime. And for some, even 2&20 isn't enough. The most successful hedge funds have argued that their very success should allow them to extract yet a greater percentage of the upside of their investments. James Simons, for instance, founder and controlling shareholder of hedge fund Renaissance Technologies, isn't satisfied with 2&20; at latest check, Renaissance charges its clients 5 percent per year for assets under management plus 36 percent carried interest. It is nothing short of breathtaking.

AN INNOCENT BEGINNING

While 2&20 had an innocent beginning with a tantalizingly logical proposition of aligning managers with investors, its utter pervasiveness raises the question: does it actually do what it purports to do? We've already seen that stock-based incentive compensation to executives, intended to align their interests with the interests of shareholders, does nothing of the sort. It instead provides a clear incentive and an explicit mechanism for executives to damage the interests of investors. Does 2&20 work any better?

It doesn't take terribly sophisticated analysis to determine that it most certainly does not. The 2&20 formula fails to align the interests of investment managers and their clients for the same fundamental reason that stock option incentives fail to align the interests of executives and shareholders—both structures align interests only on the upside and so encourage rampant risk-taking on the part of agents at the expense of principals.

Giving stock options to executives aligns the upside nicely—if the stock goes up, shareholders and option holders get rich. But if the share price goes down, the shareholders take it in the teeth and the option holders, who got their options for free in the first place, don't lose a thing. The possibility of huge upside rewards and no downside real losses means that executives are incented to undertake highly risky actions in hopes of making their options worth a fortune. If the plans don't work out so well, the executive won't be heartbroken as the existing tranche of options expires worthless. Thanks to a dropping stock price in the wake of the failed initiative, the executive will soon get a new allotment of options at a much lower price.

During the options-granting boom in the 1990s, an executive would typically earn an attractive base salary with stock options on top (plus perhaps a cash bonus plan). So the executive had a guaranteed salary income to count on, even if the options were to expire without value. But if the stock price went up, putting the options in the money, the executive would earn an unlimited, equity-like upside. Investment managers following the 2&20 formula have a strikingly similar compensation structure: they are guaranteed a 2 percent fee for assets under management—a stable sum that can pay all the bills, which they receive even if they don't produce a penny of upside for the investors. And, in addition, if they manage to earn a return for the investors, they, too, will earn an unlimited, equitylike upside. Like executives with options, these managers have clear incentive to undertake high-risk, high-reward strategies to drive upside with no need to worry about downside. The use of stock options as executive compensation fell out of favor after 2001, as boards recognized the inherent danger they posed to the firm. Yet 2&20 is still going strong.

FEEDING THE PARASITE

It is clear that 2&20 provides the wrong kind of incentive to investment managers and should be eliminated on that basis alone. But the real and truly insidious problem with 2&20 is that it provides sustenance to an industry that has no upside for the economy and has a parasitic relationship with the public capital markets—the hedge fund business.

The 2&20 formula is relatively innocuous in two big segments of the private equity world: VC and LBOs. While the 2&20 formula doesn't align the interests of investors and managers, for VC and LBO funds, the upside on the carried interest comes only with an increase in real value. The 2&20 incentive structure may cause managers of VC and LBO funds to take high risks, but managers do have to build something of value in order to reap rewards. VC fund managers need to build a start-up into a company that is real enough to take public or sell to a larger company. Those driving LBOs have to buy an asset and improve its performance enough to unload it for a profit, whether by way of sale to a larger company or through an initial public offering. At least initially, both VC and LBO firms have to build value in the real market, not the expectations market, because they mainly invest in nontraded assets. These firms have no incentive whatsoever to diminish the value of an investment asset: their incentive is the opposite.

Hedge funds are entirely different—and dangerously so. They invest in publicly traded instruments or derivatives thereof, so they are entirely creatures of the expectations market rather than the real market. They can and will invest in any financial instrument. In fact, hedge funds have gotten so sophisticated that when there isn't an available security tailored to their investing interests, they hire investment banks to create custom investment vehicles for them. Hedge funds can invest in instruments that produce value for the fund if they go up in price, but they can also engineer investments that produce value for the fund if they go down in price. That is, they can place a bet against investments—*shorting* them. John Paulson, for example, made billions by shorting subprime mortgages (with the help of investment bankers at Goldman Sachs, which created the now-notorious Abacus mortgage-derivative vehicles purely to help Paulson bet against the mortgage market). George Soros similarly made his first billion-dollar score by shorting the British pound in 1992.

What all of this means is that hedge funds are not interested in stability or steady growth. They are interested only in short-term changes in expectations; in other words, in *volatility*. The more a hedge fund investment moves in the direction of its bet, the greater the fund's carried interest. Because the 2&20 formula dictates that the bigger the price movement, the bigger the potential payoff, it means that no amount of market upheaval is either enough or too much.

Their exploitation of variability in the capital markets has made the leading hedge fund managers very, very rich. Of the sixteen billionaires in the top hundred of the *Forbes* list who made their fortunes through the 2&20 formula, twelve are hedge-fund managers. Every year for the past several years, the highest-earning Americans were hedge fund managers. Renaissance's James Simons earned $5 billion in personal compensation in 2008 and 2009 combined.[13] These were two terrible years for the economy and the stock market, but no problem for Simons. He doesn't need growth or prosperity; he just needs volatility.

THE MANUFACTURING OF VOLATILITY

In the early days of the hedge fund industry, its managers seemed content to merely exploit the variability already inherent in the capital markets. But it didn't take terribly long for hedge funds to figure out that they could make still more money by actually *producing* volatility. For instance, hedge funds wishing to place a bet that a stock (or derivative thereof) will lose value can band together with other funds to launch a *short attack* on the target stock, driving expectations down and producing the desired downward movement in the stock. The band of hedge funds creates price fluctuations that didn't have to exist, hurting other companies and investors and reaping huge rewards.

This conduct happens to be strictly illegal, but that certainly doesn't stop the hedge funds. According to court documents, in 2003, hedge fund manager Steven Cohen of SAC Capital and a group of associates are alleged to have hired a shady operative (Spyro Contogouris) to spread negative rumors about the CEO of insurer Fairfax Financial in an attempt to create downward pressure on its stock. Cohen, Contogouris, and a number of their associates are under Securities & Exchange Commission investigation and face the prospect of legal sanctions because they got caught trying to create and exploit volatility in this manner.[14]

The confluence of stock-based compensation, the 2&20 formula, and hedge fund–generated variability has created a highly unstable situation, one that creates ever spiraling volatility. Executives are learning that they too can maximize their incentive compensation through market fluctuations—and the bloody-minded ones are doing it in spades. They inflate expectations to maximize the value of their stock-based compensation, which benefits the executive, but also benefits the hedge funds, which have yet more variability to exploit. This vicious cycle has produced a volatility machine that threatens the fundamentals of American stock markets—and, in turn, the world's capital markets.

Volatility is not entirely straightforward to measure—which index, what time period, what quantitative measure? But, if the S&P 500, the broadest index of American large capitalization stocks, is used, the thirty-year periods before and after 1980, a very long timeframe, are analyzed, and the measurement used is the standard deviation of monthly returns, volatility is approximately 15 percent higher in the later period than the earlier period. Hence, in the era of shareholder value maximization, stock-based compensation, and hedge funds, investors have experienced the double whammy of lower returns *and* greater instability.

The negative effects of volatility are most obvious in a stock market crash. Consider the dot-com meltdown:

technology company executives compensated with stock options worked with 2&20 venture capital firms to hype their start-up Internet companies, setting stratospheric expectations that shot the NASDAQ up through the 5,000 barrier and ultimately produced the crash. This was a primitive form of expectations manipulation— exploiting naive analysts, naive first-time investors, and naive Internet day-traders.

The subprime meltdown was a more mature, evolved case of the forces of stock-based compensation and 2&20 incentive compensation working together. In the end, they created a discontinuity that threatened to bring down the entire U.S. financial system. Executives with stock-based compensation chased heightening expectations farther and farther out the slender tree branch; then, hedge funds and investment dealers got together to produce derivative structures that had no other purpose but to facilitate multibillion-dollar bets on whether those expectations would rise or fall—helping to snap those slender branches. The hedge funds didn't much care which way the expectations went, so long as they did so in a big way, producing the kind of volatility that generates huge upside for their carried interests.

This is the future. All the fixes put in place in the wake of the 2000–2002 meltdown did nothing to prevent the 2008–2009 meltdown. Clever people found new ways to game the game, and the regulators didn't see it coming.

Federal regulators, the markets' version of the "competition committee," acted like Major League Baseball, waiting until a crisis was irrefutable to implement a few big fixes. We would be far better off if our regulators were to act more like the National Football League, tweaking the rules almost constantly in reaction to small shifts in power that throw the state of play out of balance.

Without ongoing good governance, the players in our capital markets will grow more and more sophisticated in their ability to game the system. None of the fixes already put in place or being contemplated will forestall the next meltdown. The hedge fund industry can and will continue to generate the volatility it needs. The parasite will threaten the host once again. If the host succumbs this time, the parasites won't much care. They have billions of dollars garnered over the past decade to comfort them.

REINING IN THE HEDGE FUNDS

While it is easy to see how hedging against macro changes in exchange rates and the like can be helpful to businesses, it is hard to see how hedge funds in their current market-making form create any kind of broader societal benefit. They earn huge returns while threatening to materially damage the capital markets system that feeds them. Hedge funds are unlike VC and LBO funds in this respect: these firms can create net societal value. VC funds help small firms with entrepreneurial ideas fund their growth and without them, we might not have Apple, Genentech, eBay, Amazon, Google, and many others. While it is true that many dollars are lost when ventures fail, the world benefits when VCs help start-ups become big companies with millions of happy consumers. Similarly, LBO firms can create societal value by taking over poorly performing companies and improving them, saving real jobs in the process (for example, Snapple and Continental Airlines). As with VC funded-companies, the goal (if not always the actual outcome) is real growth and stronger performance.

Hedge funds have no such goal. They are simply and clearly traders, not builders. Hedge funds play entirely, completely, and utterly in a zero-sum game. For James Simons to make $5 billion, Renaissance Technologies had to make profits on the order of $15–$20 billion for its clients. But that means that other investors—pensioners, high-net-worth individuals, widows, and orphans, or ordinary working Americans—had to lose $15–$20 billion.

In the expectations market, for every dollar made, there is a dollar lost, whether that's from betting on NFL football games or on the collapse of the subprime mortgage industry. Nobody is better off—except Simons and his investors—and lots and lots and lots of people are worse off. Hedge funds haven't created value; they've just transferred it to their friends. James Simons does so in the cleverest possible way, making tiny profits across millions of trades, so investors don't know when they are on the losing side of a Renaissance trade. John Paulson does it in a much more obvious way, which is to cause massive pain and suffering to just a few investors.

One might argue that James Simons and John Paulson are no different than Bill Gates; after all, each is exceedingly rich thanks to a company he started. But there are fundamental differences. Gates, like him or not, is rich because he created net value for a broad swath of society. His products are worth as much or more to each customer than that customer paid for them. His products make customers' lives better and more efficient. And since Microsoft can produce its software for less money than it sells for, Microsoft is highly profitable. As its biggest shareholder, Gates became wealthy by providing a valued product to his customers. His wealth is thus derived from his creation of a positive-sum game. Microsoft is better off and its customers are too; no one needed to lose value in order for Bill Gates to get rich. Simons and Paulson, on the other hand, had to take their money from someone else. For them to get rich, their trading partners had to lose vast sums. And of course, the more naive the trading partner, the better for Simons, Paulson, and their investors.

In football as in business, the real game is a positive-sum affair—fans enjoy the pleasure of the game, players and stadium workers get paid, and owners make a profit—while the expectations game is a zero-sum affair—bettors win and bettors lose and both have to give the bookies a cut. Hedge-fund management has the same structure as bookmaking, except that the returns are higher and it is currently legal in more states!

On one side of the ledger, hedge fund managers provide zero benefit to society; on the other side, the costs are substantial. Hedge funds have contributed to the higher systematic volatility in our equity markets and have helped create one-time meltdown events in those same markets, particularly with respect to the subprime mortgage-induced crash. And worse, it is clear that some hedge funds have engaged in criminal activities to further their goals. Like the incentive-compromised CEO, these fund managers have lost their moral compass.

While the ultimate redress for hedge funds would be to ban them outright, such a course of action seems unlikely given the size and power of the industry. But, if they are going to callously damage the capital markets for their own private interests, at least we could tax them to compensate for the damage and take some of the excess profitability out of the industry.

Hedge fund taxation is almost impossibly complex because the structures of the firms are so convoluted;

there are many permutations and combinations of general partners (that is, the fund managers) and limited partners (that is, the fund investors). For instance, investors may be foreign or domestic, individuals or non-taxable entities (for example, pension funds) or taxable entities (for example, corporations). However, most commonly, the fund is structured as a partnership, which means that taxation takes place at the level of the individual general partners and limited partners. The general partners are individuals for whom the annual fee is earned as ordinary income and for whom carried interest is earned most commonly as a short-term capital gain. The limited partners are typically a combination of high-net-worth individuals, who pay taxes on the increases as short-term capital gains, and nontaxable entities that pay no taxes when the income flows to them (especially if they are clever and structure their holdings to avoid the tax on unrelated taxable business income).

The U.S. tax code has long recognized that the level of taxation on capital gains has an impact on entrepreneurial and business-building activities. Hence, for most of the twentieth century and for the twenty-first century thus far, capital gains have enjoyed more favorable tax treatment than ordinary income—that is, wages. This is particularly the case for long-term capital gains, which are at this point defined as investments with a holding period of greater than one year. Currently, individual capital gains on assets held for a period of less than one year are taxed at a rate equal to that of ordinary income—35 percent at the highest rate—while long-term capital gains are taxed at no higher than 15 percent. For corporations, capital gains are taxed at the same rates as ordinary corporate income.

Neither hedge fund investors nor managers take much advantage of the discounted long-term capital gains tax rate because their investments are weighted toward the short term. There should be no quibble with them gaining the benefit of the discounted rate for investments that are truly long term; long-term investing is good for the economy and should be encouraged.

The bigger question concerns the taxation of short-term capital gains. In contrast to longer-term capital gains, the tax code treats such gains as equivalent to other income-generating activity such as ordinary wage income. But what if the activities undertaken to produce short-term trading gains are actually demonstrably bad for the economy? What if these activities cause greater volatility in our expectations market, variability that undermines the ability of executives to create value in the real market or causes executives to attempt to manage the expectations market rather than the real market? Then, our tax system should discourage these activities by making them less economically attractive.

To protect the capital markets from parasites that would destroy their host, short-term capital gains (on holding periods of less than one year) should be taxed at a punitive rate—say 70 percent, or about double the ordinary income rate. Similarly, only 30 percent of capital losses on holding periods of less than one year should be deductible for income tax purposes. In order to ensure that the hedge funds don't simply create synthetic products or multiparty deals to circumvent the holding-period rule, it should be a criminal (not civil) offense to structure a short-term holding as a faux long-term holding for tax avoidance purposes.

In order to protect the average investor, there should be a $1 million lifetime exemption from this higher tax (and lower loss inclusion). For the first $1 million of short-term gains and losses, the ordinary income tax rate would apply. Such an exemption would ensure that the vast majority of Americans would never have to worry about short-term capital gains taxation (because only a tiny fraction of Americans accumulate more than $1 million of short-term gains or losses in their lifetime).[15] Only those who make their living on playing the short-term expectations market will feel the sting of the tax structure, and hopefully, it will make such activity less economically rewarding than building enterprises for the future.

SAVING PENSION FUNDS
FROM THEMSELVES

It's all well and good to come down hard on hedge funds, but the fact is that they have plenty of willing customers, customers who enable the zero-sum game and encourage the proliferation of 2&20. Most particularly, the impact of hedge fund–driven volatility has been deepened by the legitimization of the risky investments by our major pension funds. As pension funds have chased higher and higher returns, they have branched out from the public capital markets and into the world of private investments (euphemistically called *alternative investments* in the pension fund world).

Of course, pension funds have long participated in a form of alternative investment that is actually quite well suited to them: real estate, which offers moderate-level, stable, long-term returns perfect for stable, long-term pension liabilities. VC funds, LBO funds, and hedge funds, the growing segments of the alternative investments industry, are precisely the opposite. As short-term investments—typically self-liquidating in five years or less—they offer exceedingly variable returns ranging all the way from complete loss of capital to a home-run win. What's more, the incentive structure of private equity is dreadful for pension funds. As discussed, once they've collected their 2 percent annual fee, fund managers have the incentive to swing for the fences with the pensioners' money. If they are successful, both the fund and the pensioners do well. If they strike out, the fund still has its annual fee to pay the bills, but the pensioners have lost their retirement nest egg.

Worse even than the perverse investing incentives of hedge funds are the very real temptations that unscrupulous hedge fund managers offer to pension funds. Hedge funds live and die by the volume of assets under management, so massive pension funds, with all of those assets to invest, are deeply attractive to them. Hence, hedge funds spare no expense in encouraging pension fund managers to allocate capital to them—whether it is taking pension managers on expensive education off-sites (or more accurately, junkets), showering them with tokens of appreciation, or, in the worst of cases, actually paying these managers personal bribes to allocate their beneficiaries' capital to the hedge fund in question.

In early 2010, thirteen private equity funds, including the impeccably connected Washington, D.C.–based Carlyle Group, reached a settlement that allowed the U.S. government to collect from them some $130 million in fines related to accusations that the firms paid New York State Common Retirement Fund managers to allocate funds to them.[16] Quadrangle Group, in paying $7 million of the above settlement, admitted openly that its senior partner at the time, Steve Rattner (later the Obama administration's "car czar"), was responsible for improprieties: "We wholly disavow the conduct engaged in by Steve Rattner, who hired the New York State Comptroller's political consultant, Hank Morris, to arrange an investment from the New York State Common Retirement Fund . . . That conduct was inappropriate, wrong, and unethical." (It is worth noting that Rattner disagrees with Quadrangle's characterization of his actions.)[17]

Despite the mismatch of private equity funds and their incentive structure with the needs of pensioners, pension fund managers have increased their allocation to private equity funds, including the insidious hedge funds, over the past two decades. They have even engaged in clear illegality along with their hedge fund friends. Some leading pension funds are fighting back against the 2&20 formula, which is terrific to see. However, many pension funds need to be saved from themselves.

In part, pension funds need to be saved from themselves because many of them are monopolies. In most states, public employees have no choice as to who manages their pension account; their deductions and employer matches go directly into the hands of a monopoly provider of pension services. And, while being a monopoly often feels comfortable and secure to the monopolist, in the longer term, it is rarely good for either its customers or the monopoly itself. Over time, monopolists can't help but evolve toward serving themselves rather than serving their customers. It isn't easy to keep up a high level of effort and diligence for a customer whose contributions you will receive regardless of how hard you work.

Having a few pension fund and hedge fund managers face substantial fines or jail terms will provide some helpful discipline to the industry, but since a number of these monopoly providers seem incapable of thinking more about their pensioners than themselves, the way they are allowed to invest with private equity funds needs to be more carefully controlled.

Pension funds and fiduciary institutions generally should not be allowed to invest their beneficiaries' assets with a manager who charges them both an asset-based fee and a carried interest. They (and their manager) need to choose: asset fee or carried interest, but not both. If the pension fund manager chooses no fee, then the private equity manager experiences a downside; it will end up working for absolutely nothing if it doesn't earn a positive return for the pension fund. In such a structure, there will automatically be less swinging for the fences because funds don't have a fixed-fee safety net. If instead the pension fund manager chooses all fees and no carried interest, then we return to the era in which investment managers worked for 1 to 2 percent of assets under management and performed just fine. Either option—all carried interest or all fixed fee—is massively preferable to the twisted incentive effects of 2&20.

Perhaps a more imaginative option would be to use *fulcrum fees* rather than 2&20. In the mutual fund world, investment advisers are forbidden by Investment Company Act 205(a)(1) from charging performance-based fees. Fulcrum fees were permitted under subsequent regulations for qualified clients (that is, clients whose net worth exceeds $1.5 million and with $750,000 or more under management). These fees operate in the following manner: Fund performance is matched to a specific external benchmark. When the fund outperforms that benchmark, the management fee increases at a specified rate. However, if the fund underperforms the benchmark, the fee decreases at the same rate. Miss the benchmark by enough, and the fund managers could earn no fee at all. Such a structure provides clear upside and downside incentives that much more clearly align interests than does 2&20.[18]

PULLING BACK FROM THE BRINK

The 2&20 formula, like stock-based incentive compensation, is a bad idea hidden in the guise of compelling logic. Its origin was part of the progression of talent wresting control from capital. But, because 2&20 disaligns where it should align, its pervasiveness and power need to be curbed to protect the real markets from its deleterious effects. Curbing the pension funds' ability to feed the 2&20 beast will help out. And sucking some of the excess profitability out of the hedge fund model through taxation will also further limit the damage done by 2&20. In due course, 2&20 should go the way of executive stock options and the dodo, but that will take some time. Hence, interim steps are needed to prevent 2&20-possessed hedge funds from bringing the capital markets fully to their knees.

Yet, more even than reining in the hedge funds, what our economy needs is a more holistic framework for talent. Solely seeking to extract as much reward as possible is a weak and inauthentic goal. Unfortunately, we have created structures that make it the only logical outcome for talent, whether they be knowledge workers, executives, athletes, or actors.

The goal of maximal extraction of financial rewards has no greater meaning and serves no higher purpose. It is a goal that transfers wealth, rather than creating value. As such, we need to create a new structure that enables talent to be fairly compensated for their efforts in pursuit of truly value-creating goals. That is the challenge of the final chapter.

SIX

A BOLD VISION FOR COMPANIES AND EXECUTIVES

Never doubt that a small group of thoughtful,
committed citizens can change the world.
Indeed it is the only thing that ever has.

—Margaret Mead

In his best-selling novel *Bonfire of the Vanities*, novelist Tom Wolfe paints a touching but disturbing picture of his hero—or perhaps more properly antihero—Sherman McCoy. Sherman is a millionaire bond trader, a Manhattan Master of the Universe. A blue-blooded, thirty-eight-year old Yale graduate, he already has a co-op flat on Park Avenue with twelve-foot ceilings, a socialite wife named Judy, a perfect six-year-old daughter named Campbell, and a mistress named Maria.

Wolfe writes that one day, Campbell runs up to Sherman and earnestly asks: "Daddy . . . what do you do?" She has learned that the father of her best friend MacKenzie "makes books, and he has eighty people working for him." Campbell is anxious to report back what her daddy does: and she hopes that it is as, or more, impressive! Sherman tries to explain: "Well, I deal in bonds, sweetheart. I buy them, I sell them, I—" Campbell interrupts, less than satisfied: "What are bonds? What is deal?" Sherman struggles vainly to explain until Judy leaps into the breach with her own answer. She tells Campbell to imagine that bonds are like slices of golden cake, cakes Sherman didn't bake, but that he passes from one person to another. And every time he passes a slice, some tiny golden crumbs fall off. He collects them together and when he has collected enough crumbs, he can make a golden cake for himself.

The analogy doesn't sit well with Sherman (little crumbs!); he and Judy argue, and before long, Campbell is in tears. Campbell is distressed, it seems, not just because of the argument but because she sees that her father's profession is meaningless. He doesn't make books, he doesn't even bake cakes. He doesn't make *anything*.

Herein lies the challenge for the modern corporate executive (or bond trader or hedge fund manager) in the era of shareholder value maximization. The shareholder value framework, bolstered by stock-based compensation (or the 2&20 formula), focuses executives on creating perceived value in the expectations market rather than on creating concrete value in the real market. This shareholder value–focused framework has distressing flaws.

First, it gives executives a task that is ultimately unachievable, in that it requires that they raise other people's expectations continuously and forever. Executives either pursue an impossible goal or game the game—that is, drive expectations up or down in the short term to extract value for themselves at the expense of shareholders. Boards of directors, who are meant to protect shareholders from this kind of exploitation by executives, turn out to be largely incapable of doing so.

Second, it saps executives of their sense of authenticity. Executives know that they are playing a game they cannot win on behalf of faceless, nameless shareholders who behave unilaterally and capriciously. Like Sherman McCoy, modern executives have difficulty explaining to themselves, let alone an impressionable youngster, how it is that what they do creates value for humanity.

Shareholder value theory generates inauthentic behavior, reduces long-term returns, and increases volatility in the capital markets. Plus, it speeds the emergence of a class of firms—hedge funds—that exist solely to prey on that volatility and that create no actual value for the economy. Shareholder value simply fails as a unifying theory to produce value in business.

If the theory that has underpinned our capitalist approach for the past three decades has failed, we need a replacement—a theory that encourages authentic action, turns attention to the real market, drives long-term growth, and produces less volatility.

A first step is to pursue the goal of creating value for customers. But merely placing customers at the fore does not in itself produce authenticity in business. There is a more expansive goal executives can pursue, one that is more consistent with an authentic life and at least equally consistent with building shareholder value: They should earnestly seek to make their business a force that improves the society in which they live and work.

THE CIVIL FOUNDATION

The quality of a society is in large part a function of the laws and the norms that guide the behaviors of its members, whether individuals or constructed entities, like for-profit companies (see figure 6-1). These rules, at their best, are designed to improve the society as a whole as well as the lives of those who belong to it. For example, the law against stealing frees citizens from spending large quantities of time and other resources protecting their own property from theft.

Laws are explicitly expressed and enforced by regulatory bodies. Members of a society who do not obey its laws

FIGURE 6-1

The civil foundation

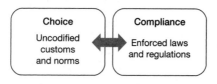

are sanctioned in some fashion. Typically, individuals who break laws are fined or jailed, while entities that transgress are fined or even disbanded. For instance, our society has laws that forbid discrimination on the basis of age, gender, religion, or sexual preference. A company that chooses to ignore those laws and to discriminate against individuals risks being fined or otherwise punished.

In addition to formal regulations, every society has shared customs and norms to which its members are expected to adhere. These norms differ from laws in that they are not codified and are largely tacit. They are also intended to make life more pleasant for society as a whole. For instance, our society has a norm that discourages taking or making phone calls during movies. Those who contravene that norm are subject to disapproval (and shushing), not to mention possible ejection by an usher.

As with regulations, there tend to be sanctions for those who do not adhere to norms. Rather than imprisonment or financial penalties, the punishment tends to be exclusion. For example, in some cities and industries, it is the norm for companies to give 1 percent of pretax profits to charity. Companies that don't contribute are excluded from activities of a formal "1 percent club" and are held in lower esteem by the community. Generally, if a company contravenes customs and norms, it may experience lower customer loyalty or have greater difficulty attracting and retaining employees.

Both laws and norms exist to make a society a better place to live. Together, they create a foundation of civility on which the society can build a spectrum of beneficial activities, including commerce, education, and the arts.

The civil foundation of any given society is not static. It evolves over time both in positive and negative directions. Often, as an economy advances, its civil foundation of laws and norms builds up. The American civil foundation, for instance, has deepened considerably over time, with huge advances in areas from stronger occupational health and safety laws for workers, to same-sex benefits for employees, to Medicare/Medicaid health care, to accounting standards, to corporate philanthropy, to name a few. Meanwhile, in numerous developing countries, the shallow and fragile civil foundation has not advanced appreciably. There, the prevailing experience is of war, use of force, dangerous working conditions, and the absence of health care. The civil foundation thus varies widely across societies—both between particular communities within a given legal jurisdiction and across jurisdictions.

Unfortunately, even in the most advanced of economies, the civil foundation does not inexorably grow stronger. Disruptions like recessions, natural disasters, terrorist attacks, or even shifting population patterns can reduce prosperity and diminish the civil foundation over time. One might argue that aspects of the civil foundations of developed countries are currently crumbling as competition from low-cost jurisdictions chips away at both employment laws and company norms for treatment of workers. For instance, a global company might choose, for the benefit of its shareholders, to locate more of its work in low-labor-cost economies. These low-cost economies tend to have a shallower civil foundation, meaning the company is shifting jobs away from a country that has a deep and robust civil foundation toward one that does not. The country with the deep foundation, facing job losses and globalization panic, might be inclined to loosen its regulations and standards—to chip away at the foundation—in order to keep jobs at home.

The civil foundation can also weaken in a climate of fear. One particularly dark moment for America's civil foundation was the internment of ethnic Japanese during World War II. America backed away from its laws and norms regarding civil liberties to target a group of

American citizens, the overwhelming majority of whom had done nothing wrong and posed no threat.

This was not an isolated or unprecedented phenomenon. John Stuart Mill commented on the influence of war on freedom in his seminal essay *On Liberty*: war, he said, fosters "a mode of thinking which may have been admissible in small republics surrounded by powerful enemies, in constant peril of being subverted by foreign attack or internal commotion, and to which even a short interval of relaxed energy and self-command might so easily be fatal that they could not afford to wait for the salutary permanent effects of freedom."[1] In general, the civil foundation strengthens during periods of calm, optimism, or prosperity and weakens during times of fear or economic contraction.

THE EVOLUTION OF THE CIVIL FOUNDATION

As major actors in modern society, companies can have a negative, neutral, or positive impact on the evolution of the civil foundation. The people who run these companies have a choice: they can chip away at the bricks of the civil foundation; they can benefit from the existing foundation but not contribute to it; or they can work to add bricks to and strengthen the robustness of the foundation. The choice executives make for their companies determines how companies are seen by society as a whole.

Executives at AIG made the civil foundation less robust through their involvement in credit default swaps. Credit derivatives aren't inherently a bad thing; they hold the promise of helping financial companies more effectively manage the risk of their portfolios. But AIG embraced credit derivatives in a dangerous and ultimately disastrous manner—taking an approach that clearly placed corporate and executive wealth ahead of our collective well-being. Chasing supernatural profits, AIG hired a group of derivatives specialists and set them up in London, where the regulatory structures happened to be less restrictive than in New York. Under U.S. laws, AIG was able to select its own regulator for the new division and, rather than the highly experienced Securities & Exchange Commission, AIG opted for the Office for Thrift Supervision, which had virtually no expertise in the credit default swap arena. The result, as Treasury Secretary Tim Geithner would later testify before Congress, was that AIG's Financial Products Group was largely unregulated. In creating this new division, AIG ventured into a business far outside its core insurance expertise and went on to leverage the trusted AIG name to lend credibility to these little-understood financial vehicles.

Rather than embrace appropriate regulatory oversight, executives at AIG did everything in their power to skirt regulations, staying within the letter of the law—even if not the spirit—while exposing AIG and its partners to colossal, little-understood risks in pursuit of massive profits. By the time the U.S. mortgage market crashed in 2008, AIG's London-based Financial Products group had entered into almost $500 billion of credit default swap agreements. The losses associated with its defaults led to the largest government bailout in U.S. history and contributed meaningfully to the worst financial crisis since the Great Depression.

In similar fashion, the executives of Enron, World-Com, and the hundreds of options-backdating companies bent or broke rules meant to build trust between investors and companies. Thankfully, such rule breakers are a small minority among executives. Few executives go so far as to engage in criminal activity, because such behavior creates dissonance with how they see themselves and with who they want to be in the rest of their lives. No parent wants to be Sherman McCoy and have their child burst into tears when they have explained to them what their parent actually does for a living.

Unfortunately, even a small number of executives who get up every morning, chisel in hand and ready to start chipping away, can do serious damage to the civil foundation. It takes a long time to rebuild, and society can't afford to stand by idly while important bricks are broken down.

Much more common than the foundation chippers are executives who seek to neither augment nor diminish the civil foundation. They subscribe to Milton Friedman's famous adage that the business of business is business. In a seminal 1970 article in the *New York Times Magazine* entitled "The Social Responsibility of a Business Is to Increase Its Profits," Friedman argued that the sole responsibility of a business is to return its profits to shareholders and that to do otherwise—to spend shareholders' money to improve social welfare, for instance—would be presumptuous, inefficient, and ineffectual. Return profits to shareholders, Freidman said, and let them spend their money as they wish. Friedman closed his article definitively, by quoting from his book *Capitalism and Freedom*: "There is one and only one social responsibility of business—to use its resources and engage in activities designed to increase its profits so long as it stays within the rules of the game, which is to say, engages in open and free competition without deception or fraud."[2]

Executives who hold to Friedman's philosophy work assiduously to ensure that their companies are in strict compliance with all the laws and regulations governing their operation, and they keep fully in line with the norms and conventions of their industry or region. If companies in their industry or region engage in corporate philanthropy, so do they—at approximately the same level of investment as their peers. If other companies adopt same-sex benefits, so do they. This kind of toeing the line is indeed helpful to society. Widespread adherence to laws and adoption of norms protects and reinforces the existing civil foundation, and that is a very good thing. It gives everyone greater confidence in the legal foundations of the society, and it spreads beneficial norms across entire industries and regions.

However, this approach does nothing to enhance the civil foundation; it simply relies on the efforts of those who established the laws and norms in the first place. At the end of one's career, who would want to say: "I ensured that my company obeyed all relevant laws and whenever other companies started doing something good for society that they didn't have to do, we followed. I did what was obvious and expected—and nothing more—for my entire career"? Many may end up in that place; but few consciously choose it from the beginning.

A SUPERIOR OPTION

There is a superior option, one that only a fraction of senior executives choose to embrace. It is to contribute to strengthening the civil foundation, going beyond the laws and regulations already in place and the norms and conventions already prevailing. This means venturing into the frontier territory of initiatives that have not yet been attempted but that hold the promise of making the world a better place. It means truly taking the lead on initiatives that mean more than profits.

Interestingly, there is a long history of companies and individuals that acted to build up the civil foundation:

- In 1914, Henry Ford, believing that he ought to pay his workers enough to afford to buy the cars they produced, more than doubled the hourly wages Ford Motor Company paid, from $2.34 to $5. He was roundly criticized by other industrialists and appeared to place himself at a disadvantage, since the wages at his plants were well in excess of the norms in the auto industry at the time. But his decision ultimately benefited his company, making it an attractive employer, reducing turnover to almost zero, and stimulating demand for its products. At the same time, Ford's move benefited society by raising the bar for pay and labor practices across the auto industry.[3]

- In 1976, Anita Roddick opened The Body Shop and demonstrated that beauty-care products could be developed without animal testing. Her approach resonated with consumers and caused competitors to fall into line or suffer the embarrassment of continuing in an unseemly and unpopular practice.

- In 1990, Prudential Insurance introduced *viatical settlements*—contracts that allowed AIDS sufferers to tap into the death benefits in their life insurance policies to pay for medical and related expenses. Favorable media reaction to this innovation convinced rival insurers that the risk of introducing similar products was negligible, and the policy became business as usual throughout the insurance industry.

- In 2009, Walmart announced its Sustainable Product Index project, a plan to create a common index for assessing the sustainability of all of its suppliers, with the intent of purchasing in part on the basis of sustainability performance.[4] Given Walmart's purchasing clout, the belief is that suppliers will have to comply with the index. If consumers respond, as well, other retailers will be inclined to follow Walmart's example, applying pressure to the retailing industry's whole supply chain and dramatically improving its sustainability.

These cases, and the others like them, have a common structure. First, an executive believes that some segment of society—whether customers, employees, or the populace in general—would be better off after a given initiative. Second, the executive believes that the initiative wouldn't hurt the company's competitiveness or share-holder value in the long run. Based on intrinsic motivation, balanced with thoughtful attention to the bottom line, the executive puts the initiative into action and, sure enough, it makes the world a better place. More than that, the initiative turns out to be not profit-neutral, but actually good for competitiveness and shareholder value. Finally, the initiative is copied by other companies, making it an industry or regional norm—that is, part of a newly enhanced civil foundation.

This is how the robustness of the civil foundation is enhanced over time through company action. To begin, an individual company undertakes an activity in the frontier. Sometimes, as that practice yields success, it is imitated until it becomes a widely adopted norm, as with Prudential's aforementioned viatical settlements. Prudential's competitors all adopted a similar practice because it made the world a better place *and* was competitively successful. Over the course of twenty years, something beneficial for society went from a glimmer of an idea to an industry norm, all because one person in one company ventured into the frontier of things that had not yet been done.

Sometimes the frontier innovation is so significant and wide-reaching that it becomes ensconced in laws or regulations. For example, only one year after Walmart introduced its Sustainable Product Index initiative, the

U.S. government put in place a regulation requiring the same type of supply chain environmental disclosure from all of its suppliers.[5]

THE LIMITS OF INDIVIDUAL ACTION

However, this kind of success is anything but a sure thing. Some initiatives in the frontier do not help the company (or anyone else) and fail utterly to strengthen the civil foundation. The venerable Massachusetts textile firm Malden Mills provides the prototypical tale. A fire destroyed its primary manufacturing plant in 1995. The $300 million insurance settlement from the fire represented an opportunity for owner Aaron Feuerstein either to rebuild his plant in Mexico or to outsource his production to China. The vast bulk of the once-thriving New England textile industry had already decamped to lower-cost jurisdictions or had gone out of business. But Feuerstein refused to follow suit, maintaining that he had a responsibility to his workers and his community. So he used the insurance proceeds to rebuild the plant in northern Massachusetts and to pay his workers while it was under construction. For the workers, this was a wonderful gesture of support. Sadly, no one except the workers really cared. Feuerstein rebuilt his plant in one of the highest-cost jurisdictions on the planet and his customers, distribution channel, and government provided no reward for doing so. In short order, Malden Mills went into Chapter 11 bankruptcy protection, as its high-cost structure rendered it completely uncompetitive.

Though Feuerstein ventured boldly into the frontier, he produced only a short-term benefit for society and did great harm to his company. By continuing to pay his employees, he spared his workers considerable hardship and relieved the state of the costs associated with increased unemployment, including unemployment insurance and welfare payments. But his generosity directly diminished his own wealth and hurt his fellow shareholders. Unlike Ford, Body Shop, and Prudential, Malden Mills' initiative was unsuccessful, and so it was not imitated. It didn't establish a new norm for American business, and in the end provided a cautionary tale about adventures in the frontier.

Malden Mills was unable to turn the proverbial tide. While some customers rued the loss of American jobs, this sentiment alone didn't motivate them to reward Malden Mills for bucking the trend toward production in low-cost jurisdictions. Customers were unwilling to pay more money for products of equal quality simply because they were produced in New England. Ford, Body Shop, and Prudential each captured substantial benefits from their initiatives for themselves, through decreased employee turnover, higher customer loyalty, or greater customer appeal. In contrast, none of the benefits created by Malden Mills accrued to its shareholders.

A more recent example of the challenges of attempting to produce change by venturing alone into the frontier is BP. In 2000, CEO John Browne announced that the new positioning for BP PLC would be "Beyond Petroleum." The new BP used a stylized flower as its logo, signaling that its intent was to move beyond dependence on petroleum into a world of alternative fuels. BP backed up this positioning in 2005 with the establishment of an Alternative Energy Division to invest in nonpetroleum-based energy sources. However, the division was put up for sale just three years later, having invested only $1.5 billion in alternative energy projects, a small fraction of BP's total investment in energy production.[6] In 2008, under new CEO Tony Hayward, the Beyond Petroleum tagline disappeared and BP made a large investment in the Alberta tar sands, whose development is considered by many environmentalists to be an ecological disaster. Long before the 2010 *Deepwater Horizon* debacle, BP was in full-scale retreat from the frontier. It had nothing to show for its efforts except a reputation for being disingenuous.

Moving from a focus on oil to one on alternative energy was a huge challenge for a single company—even a large energy company. To be successful, BP would have had to change the course of energy investment and production across the industry. The costs were enormous and the returns simply too uncertain. It was unclear how much of

FIGURE 6-2

The frontier

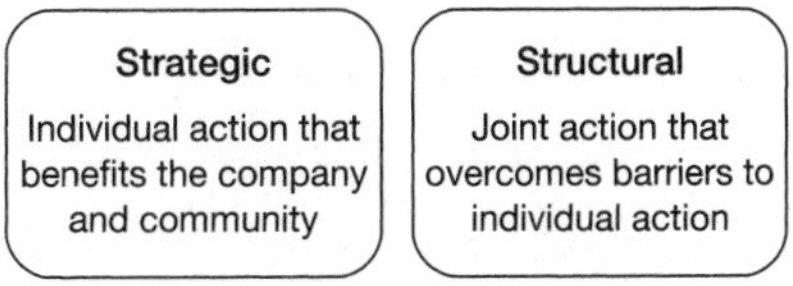

Strategic	Structural
Individual action that benefits the company and community	Joint action that overcomes barriers to individual action

the benefit of the shift to renewable fuel sources would accrue to BP and how much to those external to BP.

A fundamentally different approach is required when not enough of the benefits of individual action can be captured to make up for the costs incurred, as was the case for Malden Mills and BP. When the benefits to innovative action in the frontier accrue to actors outside the initiating company—whether to competitors in general or society as a whole—and don't benefit the company at a level in excess of the costs of innovation, the company would be foolhardy to act alone. In such an instance, joint action is required.

JOINT ACTION IN THE FRONTIER

Fortunately, there is precedent for joint company action in the frontier. In 2002, the global cement industry had reached a crossroads. The industry had come to understand that, even though it was tiny in terms of assets and revenues, it was generating approximately 5 percent of the world's man-made carbon dioxide. No single cement company could make a big dent in the situation alone and, even if one could, the level of investment required was likely to make that company uncompetitive—it would have substantially higher costs, and it was unlikely that customers would reward it for its actions. Sadly, for customers, cement is cement!

Yet, at the same time, if companies took no action, the industry would continue to be a disproportionate contributor to environmental degradation, which was unappealing on its face, but also increased the possibility that the government would step in with potentially draconian regulations to enforce change. So ten of the world's largest cement manufacturers joined together, facilitated by the World Business Council for Sustainable Development (WBCSD), to create the Cement Sustainability Initiative.[7] The joint initiative provided three major benefits that individual action could not. First, the ten companies together had the resources necessary to tackle the problem at the scale required, in contrast to Malden Mills and BP. Second, none of the participating companies was disadvantaged in relation to the others, because all of their major competitors were making proportionate investments. And third, while the benefits internal to any one company might not be clearly identifiable, the benefits to the industry as a whole were potentially great.

A more recent example of joint action in the frontier is the Eco-Patent Commons, which was established in January of 2008 by IBM, Nokia, Pitney Bowes, and Sony, once again with the WBCSD facilitating. The founding companies agreed to contribute their patents relating to environmental innovations to an open patent pool that could be used by any company or individual. Their hope in creating the pool is that other companies will follow, enriching the pool and enabling increased innovation in environmental sustainability.[8]

AN INSPIRING AND AUTHENTIC LIFE

The civil foundation and the frontier are both critical elements to the creation of meaning in business. Together, they form a matrix—what might be called the *virtue matrix*—that can be used to parse the broader social meaning of business.[9] Using this framework, business executives can think about acting in a way that is conducive to an inspiring and authentic life and wholly consistent with creating value for shareholders.

The first task is to protect the civil foundation as it currently exists. With respect to laws and regulations pertinent to the company, committed executives ensure that mechanisms are in place to guarantee that their company is in absolute compliance with both the letter and the spirit of each law and every regulation. With respect to norms and conventions pertinent to a company's industry or region, committed executives ensure that their company takes a leading rather than laggardly position in adopting those norms and conventions. By complying thoroughly with laws and regulations and fully embracing norms and conventions, a company contributes to maintaining the strength of the civil foundation—which is an important contribution to its society. By contributing to society in this way, executives create a personal sense of authenticity; they stand along with the community, not in opposition or indifferent to it.

The second and most aspirational task is to contribute meaningfully to ratcheting up the strength of the civil foundation. This can come about through either individual action or joint action, depending on the circumstances.

Some potential individual activities hold promise to make the world a better place and contribute to shareholder value by generating positive reactions from customers, employees, and/or legal authorities. These activities have potential for high impact because, if they are successful, other companies tend to imitate the innovator until the practice becomes a norm. In other words, successful individual action in the frontier can eventually become part of the civil foundation. This shift to the civil foundation provides the greatest benefit to society, in that it dramatically magnifies the impact of a single company's actions.

Executives committed to adding bricks to the civil foundation ensure that at all times their company has at least one strategic project under way that represents bold and pioneering social action. Because innovation is always risky, some such projects will fail and some will succeed. Customers will respond to some and not to others. The key is to relentlessly pursue projects in the frontier to develop a track record there. Over time, executives and companies that establish a record of success in the frontier become known in their industry and beyond as innovative and responsible. They garner reputations for making periodic breakthroughs that lead to the establishment of new conventions. For example, through concerted, ongoing initiatives, the Body Shop is recognized as a leader in sustainability and social responsibility, attracting loyal customers who shop there as much because of its reputation as because of its products.

Not all issues respond well to individual action; some are too big or costly to yield to a single company's efforts without damaging that company, creating a fundamental structural barrier to corporate action. In these cases, joint action is required. In addition to individual strategic initiatives, executives committed to shoring up the civil foundation ensure that at all times their company is pursuing at least one project jointly with other companies where the benefits of the initiative accrue principally to society rather than to the innovating company. In such situations, executives can play an initiating role in creating a coalition for action. As these initiatives succeed, the lead companies and executives become known in their industry and beyond as collaborative and cooperative. They garner reputations for leading breakthroughs in areas that foil individual company initiatives. In the case of the Cement Sustainability Initiative, the leading role of Dutch cement giant Holcim is recognized, as is its CEO of the day, Thomas Schmidheiny.

Over time, joint initiatives to pursue structural problems can become part of the civil foundation too; as jurisdictions recognize the value of the initiatives, they may enshrine the new rules as laws that apply to all firms, not just those that undertook the joint action. Here, too, the civil foundation is strengthened.

To return briefly to the example of the NFL, we can see both strategic and structural initiatives in action. At a company level, every team engages in individual strategic initiatives, the kind of community engagement and philanthropic activity that fosters loyalty and creates a hometown fan base. Individual players host fundraising events, the front office donates merchandise and tickets to worthy causes, and the team works with community groups in a variety of other ways. The Indianapolis Colts, for instance, have a program called Colts Community Tuesdays, in which players and personnel participate in worthy events every Tuesday of the season. Events include an annual Bleed Blue Blood Drive at Lucas Oil Stadium, hospital visits, Christmas caroling, and so on.

But the league takes collective action as well to generate the kind of national impact that it would be too costly and logistically complex for any one team to undertake. The flagship program of this type is NFL Play60. Created in partnership with the United Way, Play60 targets the problem of childhood obesity. Designed to promote healthier lives for kids, the program encourages children to be active at least sixty minutes each day. The league leads the initiative, and asks players and teams to support it with public service announcements, playground-building projects, and fitness camps. In this way, the NFL engages both strategic and structural initiatives in the frontier.

It is through such individual and joint innovations that the civil foundation of a society is strengthened and that society advances as a result; what were once dreams become possibilities and, eventually, reality.

If there is no innovation by executives and companies, the civil foundation will grow slowly. Governments will build the foundation up by creating new laws and regulations. Social entrepreneurs will explore the frontier and start trends that eventually end up in the foundation. But this will produce a society that can't count on business to do anything other than conduct business. While this is not a disaster, it is hardly an inspiring vision for business corporately or its executive leaders personally.

If all companies engaged in both protection and enhancement of the civil foundation, business would be (and would be seen to be) a positive agent for change in the world. Business would become skilled at strengthening the civil foundation, while earning an attractive return for shareholders, instead of becoming skilled at sacrificing everything necessary to make this quarter's earnings forecast.

If executives engaged in both protecting and strengthening the civil foundation, they would lead more authentic lives and contribute meaningfully to their communities. In the current construct, executives have a business life that is substantially detached from and at odds with their home life. This divide is untenable. People don't want to be indifferent to their community; they want to be valuable members of a community that they value and that is valued by others. Executives can make their business life consistent with their nonbusiness life and be authentic to their true selves if they set a personal goal of contributing to the strength and stability of the civil foundation.

Imagine if all executives sought to contribute in their own small way, while earning the shareholders who provided capital to their company a return above their cost of capital. That would be a worthy goal. That would bring true meaning to the firm. If executives and companies set that as their goal, they would contribute to making the world a better place—one little step at a time. It may not look or feel massively heroic, but such action would be sustainable for them, their companies, and the world.

LOOKING AHEAD

The world is a crowded, politically unstable, and economically inequitable place. The prosperity of its inhabitants depends in considerable part on the rational and responsible creation of wealth through the operation of successful businesses. Sadly, the advent of shareholder value theory and the structures that have taken shape in its wake—including stock-based incentive compensation, the 2&20 formula, and hedge funds—have delegitimized capital markets and cast a shadow over capitalism itself. This, in turn, makes it difficult for creative and entrepreneurial people to find their meaning in business. But productive action is possible, individually and communally. In part, we can learn from the NFL just what to do. We can begin by keeping our players from betting on the games they play. We can provide the right incentives to our executives—returning the focus to the real market and away from the expectations market. Like Pete Rozelle and his successors, we can endeavor to consistently tweak the rules to keep our fans happy, focusing our executives on customer delight rather than share-holder value.

Beyond the lessons of the NFL, we can make significant changes to rules that govern the players who bridge between the real and expectations markets. We can rethink the role of boards, and create the right incentives there too. We can change our attitude toward expectations market players that exist only to extract value from the world, by taxing the profits from short-term trading to all of our benefit. Finally, we can provide a framework that enables companies and executives to think about their responsibilities beyond shareholders.

In so doing, we can restore the core of business and capitalism. We can fix the game—until the next time we need to tweak it!

NOTES

Chapter One

1. Robert Shiller's online data: http://www.econ.yale.edu/~shiller/data.htm.

2. Chris Gaither and Dawn C. Chmielewski, "Fears of Dot-Com Crash, Version 2.0," *Los Angeles Times*, July 16, 2006.

3. Bethany McLeand and Peter Elkind, "The Guiltiest Guys in the Room," CNNMoney, July 5, 2006, http://money.cnn.com/2006/05/29/news/enron_guiltyest/index.htm; http://www.newsweek.com/ 2002/01/21/who-killed-enron.html#.

4. J. Michael Anderson, *Enron: A Select Chronology of Congressional, Corporate, and Government Activities* (Washington, DC: Congressional Research Service, Library of Congress, April 9, 2003).

5. Bob Dart, "Enron Chief Vilified Amid Senate Scorn, Lay Takes the 5th," *Atlanta Journal-Constitution*, February 13, 2002.

6. Laura Goldberg, "Being 'in the Dark' Could Be Asset to Former Enron Chairman's Case," *Houston Chronicle*, February 15, 2002.

7. Michael C. Jensen and William H. Meckling, "Theory of the Firm: Managerial Behavior, Agency Costs and Ownership Structure," *Journal of Financial Economics* 3, no. 4 (1976): 305–360.

8. My criticism of the application of the theory is not intended to be a critique of Jensen and Meckling as scholars or to diminish their contributions. Jensen and Meckling identified a real and pervasive problem—that the incentives of shareholders and executives are not naturally

aligned. Unfortunately, as the theory was put into practice, especially as concerns the best way to align those interests, it has served to exacerbate rather than cure the problems its authors identified. Sadly, Meckling passed away in 1998. However, Jensen has continued to be a prolific researcher and writer. His recent work highlights the role of authentic leadership in overcoming the management behavior problems identified in his original agency theory work.

9. How do we know that a stock price is much more about future expectations than it is about current real market performance? Since the inception of the S&P 500 index in 1871, it has traded on average at a price-earnings multiple of approximately sixteen times (see Robert Shiller's online data: http://www.econ.yale.edu/~shiller/data. htm). That means that an investor in the S&P 500 pays 6 percent (that is, one-sixteenth) of the price of the stock for what is happening now—current real earnings—and 94 percent for what stock investors collectively expect the company to do in the future.

10. Michael C. Jensen, Kevin J. Murphy, and Eric G. Wruck, "Remuneration: Where We've Been, How We Got to Here, What Are the Problems, and How to Fix Them," working paper, Social Science Research Network, July 12, 2004, http://ssrn.com/abstract=561305.

11. Scott Thurm, "Oracle's Ellison: Pay King," *Wall Street Journal*, July 27, 2010, http://online.wsj.com/article/SB10001424052748703724104575379680484726298.html.

12. http://people.forbes.com/profile/ray-r-irani/46931.

13. Michael Hiestand, "NFL Getting Fortunate Bounces," *USA Today,* October 30, 2009.

14. http://www.associatedcontent.com/article/2681255/2010_super_bowl_becomes_most_watched.html.

15. Tom Van Riper, "Valuations: The Most Valuable Teams in Sports," Forbes.com: http://forbes.com/2010/01/12/manchester-united-yankees-cowboys-business-sports-valuable-teams.html.

16. Again in 1983, Rozelle indefinitely suspended an NFL player (Baltimore Colts quarterback Art Schlichter) for gambling on sports events, though apparently not on NFL games. After another incident, Rozelle banned Schlichter permanently from the NFL.

17. Eli Bartov, Dan Givoly, and Carla Hayn, "The Rewards to Meeting or Beating Earnings Expectations," *Journal of Accounting and Economics* 33 (2002): 173–204.

18. Or almost perfect, anyway: while the Patriots went undefeated in the regular season, they lost to the New York Giants in the Super Bowl. Only the 1972 Miami Dolphins have a perfect record, including both regular season (then fourteen games) and playoffs (two games).

19. http://www.goldsheet.com/gs_new/histnfl.php.

20. Ibid.

21. Roger Martin, "Reward Real Growth, Not Expectations," *Financial Times*, August 2, 2010.

22. http://www.finance.yahoo.com/q/hp?s=CSCO+Historical+Prices.

23. Paul Brent, "The Real Cost of the House That Jack Built," *National Post*, September 7, 2002.

24. CAGR calculated on S&P returns adjusted for inflation and dividends, using Bloomberg LP terminal data in January 2010.

25. "2008 Hedge Fund Rich List," *Absolute Return + Alpha* magazine, http://www.marketfolly.com/2009/03/top-25-highest-paid-hedge-fund-managers.html

26. Of course, hedging can be a sensible and prudent investment strategy, one that makes a good deal of sense for handling foreign exchange risk and other macro-economic factors. In this book, I'm referring not to the practice of hedging against risk, but to the majority of the modern hedge funds, which do not exist to hedge risk but rather to make naked bets on price movements.

Chapter Two

1. Tim Webb, "BP's Boss Admits Job on the Line over Gulf Oil Spill," *Guardian*, May 14, 2010, http://www.guardian.co.uk/business/2010/may/13/bp-boss-admits-mistakes-gulf-oil-spill.

2. "Embattled BP Chief: I Want My Life Back," TimesOnline.com, http://business.timesonline.co.uk/tol/business/industry_sectors/natural_resources/article7141137.ece.

3. http://www.bp.com/sectiongenericarticle.do?categoryId=9002630&contentId=7005204.

4. "FT Global 500 2010," http://media.ft.com/cms/66ce3362-68b9-11df-96f1-00144feab49a.pdf.

5. http://www.pg.com/en_US/company/purpose_people/index.shtml.

6. James C. Collins and Jerry I. Porras, "Organizational Vision and Visionary Organizations," *California Management Review* 34, no. 1 (1991): 30–52.

7. Liam Cassidy, "Apple Shareholder's Meeting Roundup," gigacom, February 26, 2010, http://gigaom.com/apple/apple-shareholders-meeting-roundup/.

8. Peter Burrows, "Options Expert Erik Lie, on Apple's Backdating Disclosures," *BusinessWeek*, December 30, 2006, http://www.businessweek.com/technology/ByteOfTheApple/blog/archives/2006/12/u.html.

9. "Procter & Gamble Settles a Toxic Shock Suit," *New York Times*, August 25, 1982, http://www.nytimes.com/1982/08/25/us/procter-gamble-settles-a-toxic-shock-suit.html.

10. "J&J Recalls More Products After Unusual Odor," Reuters, http://www.reuters.com/article/idUSTRE60E2L420100115.

11. My colleague Mihnea Moldoveanu, who understands optimization theory as well as anyone I know, points out that it is technically possible to optimize two things at once, though to do so is both computationally complex and organizationally impractical on an ongoing basis.

12. Roger Martin and Mihnea Moldoveanu, "Capital Versus Talent: The Battle That's Reshaping Business," *Harvard Business Review*, July 2003, 36–41.

13. Ibid.

14. Adolf A. Berle and Gardiner C. Means, *The Modern Corporation and Private Property* (New York: Macmillan Co., 1933).

15. CAGR calculated on S&P returns adjusted for inflation and dividends, using Bloomberg LP terminal data in January 2010.

16. Roger Martin, "The Age of Customer Capitalism," *Harvard Business Review*, January–February 2010, 58–65. Calculated from Bloomberg data.

17. Ibid.

18. Owen Linzmayer and Brian Chaffin, "Apple Goes Public, 1984 Airs," December 16, 2004, http://www.macobserver.com/columns/thisweek/2004/20041218.shtml.

19. In fact, Microsoft had thrown Apple a $150 million lifeline to keep the company afloat in the early days of Jobs's return.

20. A battle is brewing in 2011 as well. If the league takes a consistent approach, it will fight hard to avoid giving up the gains of the past three decades.

21. In the late 1990s, the NFL tweaked its agreement for the equal sharing of television revenue, creating a pool of capital to be invested in the construction of new stadiums. In coordination with team owners, the league was able to help produce new (or dramatically reconstructed) stadiums in Chicago, Denver, Green Bay, New Oleans, New England, Philadelphia, and Seattle. This change to the revenue sharing rules helped spur the largest infusion of private investment in stadium construction in the league's history.

22. http://www.databasefootball.com/.

23. In fact, Parcells' former assistants, including Bill Belichick, Tom Coughlin, and Sean Payton, have gone on to win five additional Super Bowls as head coaches through 2010.

24. Tom Van Riper, "The Most Valuable Teams in Sports," Forbes. com, http://www.forbes.com/2009/01/13/nfl-cowboys-yankees-biz-media-cx_tvr_0113values.html.

25. Of course, not all capital is raised in a company's initial public offering. Successful companies typically issue further equity at higher prices based on success in the real market, which in turn fuels higher prices in the expectations market. For example, a company goes public at $10 per share and experiences success that pushes the stock to $30 per share. That company then decides it needs more capital and issues equity at $30 per share. In that case, management should feel the feel the obligation to earn a return for all shareholders at or above the cost of equity on the $30 per share price. There is only one class of common shares, and the company can't distinguish between one common shareholder and the next, so it needs to earn a return on the $30 per share level for all shareholders. Such a rule provides good discipline for management; it has to want additional capital badly enough to ratchet up its return requirement substantially (in this case, three times) on its original capital. This model would give management pause to consider whether it really needs and wants additional capital.

Chapter Three

1. For comparison's sake, the paid circulation of *Harvard Business Review* is 235,000, according to data from the Audit Bureau of Circulations, June 2008.

2. Erik Lie, "On the Timing of CEO Stock Option Awards," *Management Science* 51, no. 5 (2005): 802–812.

3. David Yermack, "Good Timing: CEO Stock Option Awards and Company News Announcements," *Journal of Finance* 52, no. 2 (1997): 449–476.

4. Mark Maremont, "Authorities Probe Improper Backdating of Options," *Wall Street Journal*, November 11, 2005.

5. "The Time 100," *Time*, May 3, 2007.

6. Dan Macsai, "Powerful Profs," *BusinessWeek*, August 22, 2007.

7. Peter Lattman, "Prosecutions in Backdating Scandal Bring Mixed Results," *New York Times*, November 12, 2010.

8. Ibid.

9. http://www.gallup.com/poll/1654/Honesty-Ethics-Professions. aspx.

10. Eli Bartov, Dan Givoly, and Carla Hayn, "The Rewards to Meeting or Beating Analysts' Earnings Forecasts," *Journal of Accounting and Economics* 33, no. 2 (2002): 173–204.

11. Matt Krantz and Jon Swartz, "Dell Settles SEC Charges of Playing Accounting Rules," *USA Today*, July 23, 2010.

12. Bartov, Givoly, and Hayn, "The Rewards to Meeting or Beating Analysts' Earnings Forecasts."

13. Michael C. Jensen, "The Agency Costs of Overvalued Equity and the Current State of Corporate Finance," *European Financial Management* 10, no. 4 (2004): 549–565.

14. Justin Fox, "Learn to Play the Earnings Game (and Wall Street Will Love You)," *Fortune*, March 31, 1997.

15. John R. Graham, Campbell R. Harvey, and Shiva Rajgopal, "The Economic Implications of Corporate Financial Reporting," *Journal of Accounting and Economics* 40, nos. 1–3 (2005): 3–73.

16. Michael Wilbon, "Follow the Leader," *Washington Post*, February 3, 2010.

17. Given how well the happiness equation can work for a star athlete, it's easy to see how painful it can be for that athlete upon retirement: He abruptly ceases to be a valued member of his community (his team), feels marginalized from the community that he valued, and finds himself the member of a much less valued community—retired athletes, rather than current stars. His happiness equation is likely to fall apart entirely.

18. "The Fortune 500, 2010, and 1960," http://money.cnn.com/magazines/fortune/global500/2010/full_list/ and http://money.cnn.com/magazines/fortune/fortune500_archive/full/1960/.

19. Bartov, Givoly, and Hayn, "The Rewards to Meeting or Beating Analysts' Earnings Forecasts."

20. Tim Arango, "How the AOL-Time Warner Merger Went So Wrong," *New York Times*, January 10, 2010, http://www.nytimes.com/2010/01/11/business/media/11merger.html.

21. http://www.secinfo.com/dSm4r.5Aq.htm.

22. Alastair Barr, "Short-Sale Ban Disrupts Trades for Hedge Funds," MarketWatch, September 26, 2008, http://www.marketwatch.com/story/hedge-funds-suffer-as-short-selling-ban-disrupts-strategies; and "Naked Short Sales Hint Fraud in Bringing Down Lehman," Bloomberg, http://www.bloomberg.com/apps/news?pid=news archive& sid=aB1jlqmFOTCA.

23. http://money.cnn.com/galleries/2007/fortune/0711/gallery.power_25.fortune/16.html.

24. Except in the case of family-owned or closely controlled companies.

25. Bruce Springsteen, "It's Hard to Be a Saint in the City," from *Greetings from Asbury Park, N.J.*, Columbia Records, 1973.

26. This letter can be found in Václav Havel, *Open Letters: Selected Writings 1965–1990* (New York: Vintage Books, 1992).

27. Joseph Fuller and Michael C. Jensen, "Just Say No to Wall Street: Putting a Stop to the Earnings Game," *Journal of Applied Corporate Finance* 14, no. 4 (2002): 41–46.

28. Aspen Institute Corporate Values Strategy Group, *Overcoming Short-termism: A Call for a More Responsible Approach to Investment and Business Management* (Queenstown, MD: Aspen Institute, 2009).

29. Bartov, Givoly, and Hayn, "The Rewards to Meeting or Beating Analysts' Earnings Forecasts."

30. Michael C. Jensen, Kevin J. Murphy, and Eric G. Wruck, "Remuneration: Where We've Been, How We Got to Here, What Are the Problems, and How to Fix Them," working paper (Rochester, NY: SSRN, 2004), http://ssrn.com/abstract=561305.

31. Ibid.

32. Michael Beer and Nancy Katz, "Do Incentives Work? The Perceptions of a Worldwide Sample of Senior Executives," *Human Resource Planning* 26 (2003): 30–44.

33. Donald Roy, "Quota Restriction and Goldbricking in a Machine Shop," *American Journal of Sociology* 57, no. 5 (1952): 427–442.

34. "Sears, Roebuck Faces Lawsuit Contending Fraud by Tire Unit," *New York Times*, June 17, 1999.

NOTES

Chapter Four

1. http://blog.nielsen.com/nielsenwire/media_entertainment/mlb-world-series-preview-historical-us-tv-ratings/.

2. http://www.sportsmediawatch.net/2010/11/2010-world-series-tied-as-lowest-rated.html.

3. Michael Hiestand, "NFL Getting Fortunate Bounces," *USA Today*, October 30, 2009.

4. Mark Maske, "With Television Ratings on the Rise and Attendance Flagging, NFL Faces a Business Dilemma," *Washington Post*, September 19, 2010, http://www.washingtonpost.com/wp-dyn/content/article/2010/09/18/AR2010091803691.html; and http://www.sportsbusinessnews.com/_news/news_347260.php.

5. Tom Van Riper, "The Most Valuable Teams in Sports," Forbes.com: http://www.forbes.com/2009/01/13/nfl-cowboys-yankees-biz-media-cx_tvr_0113values.html.

6. Bryan Curtis, "The National Pastime(s)," *New York Times*, January 31, 2009, http://www.nytimes.com/2009/02/01/weekinreview/01curtis.html.

7. Dennis Tuttle, "Leveling the Playing Field: Moaning About Pitcher's Mounds Is in Vogue This Season," *The Sporting News*, June 30, 2003.

8. Mark Newman, "This Year in Baseball Awards Unveiled Tonight," MLB.com, December 17, 2010, http://mlb.mlb.com/index. jsp.

9. http://www.databasefootball.com/.

10. "WorldCom Fraud Centered on Connection Charges," TheStreet.com, June 27, 2002, http://www.thestreet.com/story/10029290/worldcom-fraud-centered-on-connection-costs.html.

11. Roger Martin, "The Coming Corporate Revolt," *John F. Kennedy School of Government Compass Journal* (Fall 2003).

12. Francis Fukuyama, *Trust: The Social Virtues and the Creation of Prosperity* (New York: The Free Press, 1995).

Chapter Five

1. Dave Anderson, "Sports of the Times: Being Mickey Mantle," *New York Times*, March 16, 1994, http://select.nytimes.com/gst/abstract.html?res=FA0714FF35590C758DDDAA0894DC494D81&ref=mickey_mantle.

2. Ronald Blum, "Salaries Soared, According to Annual Survey," http://www.usatoday.com/sports/baseball/mlbfs90.htm.

3. http://www.cbssports.com/mlb/salaries/top50; http://www.cbs sports.com/mlb/salaries/avgsalaries.

4. http://nbcsports.msnbc.com/id/36604848/ns/sports-nfl/.

5. Adrian Dater, "Free-Agent Contract Skyrocket, but What's the Payoff?" *Denver Post*, July 7, 2010, http://www.denverpost.com/nuggets/ci_15453693.

6. "Rodriguez Finalizes $275M Deal with Yankees," http://sports.espn.go.com/mlb/news/story?id=3153171.

7. http://content.usatoday.com/communities/thehuddle/post/2010/09/patriots-owner-robert-kraft-pleased-contract-with-tom-brady-finally-done/1.

8. http://www.boxofficemojo.com/movies/?page=releases&id=starwars4.htm; http://boxofficemojo.com/alltime/adjusted.htm.

9. Geoffrey McNab, "100 Years of Movie Stars: 1910–1929," *The Independent*, http://www.independent.co.uk/arts-entertainment/films/features/100-years-of-movie-stars-19101929-1876290.html.

10. Dorothy Pomerantz, "DiCaprio to Bank Dreamy Paycheck from 'Inception'," *Forbes*, August 10, 2010, http://www.forbes.com/2010/08/10/leonardo-dicaprio-inception-business-entertainment-dicaprio.html.

11. Then there are the managers of "Funds of Funds." These managers invest in a suite of funds, all of which extract 2&20 fees from their investors. The fund of funds managers then charge their own investors 1 percent of assets under management and 10 percent carried interest. Thus, while at first blush it appears that they charge less than 2&20, the two layers of "aligned" managers actually charge the client more—a fee of 3&30.

12. "The 400 Richest Americans 2010," *Forbes*, September 2010.

13. "2008 Hedge Fund Rich List and 2009 Hedge Fund Rich List," *Absolute Return + Alpha* magazine, http://www.marketfolly.com/2009/03/top-25-highest-paid-hedge-fund-managers.html and http://news.hereisthecity.com/news/business_news/10304.cntns.

14. Third Amended Complaint, Superior Court of New Jersey Law Division, Docket No. MRS-L-2032-06; and Tom McGinty and Kara Scannel, "SEC Looks at Hedge Funds' Trades," *Wall Street Journal*, February 13, 2009.

15. Of course, the exact amounts of the tax rates and threshold could be debated at length, and in any case would be subject to adjustment by government over time.

16. Tomoeh Murakami Tse, "New York Reaches $7 Million Settlement in Alleged Pension-fund Scandal," *Washington Post*, April 16, 2010.

17. Ibid.

18. Thanks to my Rotman School of Management colleague, Susan Christofferson, for introducing me to fulcrum fees.

Chapter Six

1. John Stuart Mill, *On Liberty* (London: Longman, Roberts & Green, 1869).

2. Milton Friedman, "The Social Responsibility of Business Is to Increase Its Profits," *New York Times Magazine*, September 13, 1970.

3. Ford wasn't all corporate virtue, unfortunately. Among other things, he used lethal tactics in breaking the 1937 strike at the Rouge River plant in Dearborn, Michigan, and he was reported to be intensely anti-Semitic.

4. http://walmartstores.com/pressroom/news/9277.aspx.

5. Tom Spoth, "GSA to Vendors: Go Green or Else," Federal-Times. com, July 12, 2010, http://www.federaltimes.com/article/20100712/ACQUISITION01/7120301/1001.

6. Robert Lea, "BP May Sell Off Green Energy Interests," *Evening Standard*, February 27, 2008, http://www.thisismoney.co.uk/markets/ article. html?in_article_id=431272&in_page_id=3.

7. *The Cement Sustainability Initiative: Our Agenda for Action*, World Business Council for Sustainable Development, July 2002.

8. Mary Tripsas, "Everybody in the Pool of Green Innovation," *New York Times*, November 1, 2009.

9. For further reading on the virtue matrix, see Roger L. Martin, "The Virtue Matrix: Calculating the Return on Corporate Responsibility," *Harvard Business Review*, March 2002, 68–75.

INDEX

Enron, 2–5, 35, 93, 141, 200
    board at, 143, 144
equity analysts, 108–109
ethics. *See also* authenticity;
        society
    boards and, 140–142, 143–144
    at Boeing, 113–114
    community and, 100–103,
        104–107, 113–114
    Enron and, 2–4
    financial incentives and, 125
    hedge funds and, 181, 186–187
    inauthenticity and, 100
    mortgage scandal and,
        114–115
    public perception of business,
        93–94
    real versus expectations
        markets and, 32–33
    shorting and, 173–174
    stock-based compensation
        and, 121–123
executives. *See also* compensation
    agency theory on, 61–62
    asking the right questions
        about, 8–10
    board dealings with, 139–145
    civil foundation strengthening
        by, 212–217
    community and, 104–116
    compensation of, 5–7,
        121–123, 158–159
    earnings management by,
        94–100
    ethics of, 3–5, 93–94
    expectations manipulation
        by, 21–26, 81–82
    inauthenticity in, 33–34, 87–129

liability of, 6
    owners versus professionals, 158
    powerful objectives and,
        70–71
    Sarbanes-Oxley on, 6
    shareholder value and,
        21–26, 193
    vision for, 191–218
expectations market. *See also*
        real market
    boards and, 137–139, 155–156
    capital markets versus, 58–60
    changing, 217–218
    as community, 107–116
    customer focus and, 56–60
    customer focus versus, 80–85
    definition of, 12
    earnings forecasts and, 20–21,
        123–124
    earnings management and,
        94–100
    executive behavior and, 27–30
    fair returns versus, 83–85
    focus in, 31–37, 37–38
    inauthenticity in, 33–34,
        119–123
    limits of, 21–26, 57–60
    long-term growth and, 32–33
    manipulating, 27–28
    meaning and, 33
    NFL, 14–21
    real performance versus,
        98–99, 179–180
    regulating, 40
    separating from real market,
        80–85
    shareholder value maximiza-
        tion and, 21–26

ACKNOWLEDGMENTS

As always, I am deeply indebted to many people for their contributions to this book. All of my books are labors of love, and it is wonderful to have the help of many colleagues, friends, and supporters along the journey.

In the case of *Fixing the Game,* the greatest thanks go to my friend, colleague, and editor-in-chief of the book, Jennifer Riel. Jennifer edits most of my work these days, coauthors some of it, and was the primary editor for this book. She and I share a passion for NFL football (although her wild enthusiasm for Peyton Manning and under appreciation of Tom Brady is problematic—but we won't go there), so it was a pleasure to work with her on fleshing out the NFL metaphor that is woven throughout the book. She is a wonderful thinker and writer and is able to keep my logic flowing without the repetition, detours, and general inelegance that would otherwise creep in. Thanks so much, Jennifer.

A number of researchers supported Jennifer's work. First among them was Darren Karn, who among other things fact-checked the whole book. Arup Ganguly provided comparative total shareholder returns data. My business school friend Jamie Anderson helped with data on investment bank fees. Rotman School chief librarian Sean Forbes was there for me any time I needed to track down data or sources, as he has been for each of my books—thanks for the long-term support, Sean. Two of our wonderful finance professors at the Rotman School helped out: I asked Tom McCurdy for help analyzing changes in market volatility over time, and he provided that research for me; and a hallway conversation with Susan Christofferson led her to provide me with an insight regarding fulcrum fees in mutual funds—a very interesting regulatory twist about which I would not have otherwise been aware. It is wonderful to have colleagues like Tom and Susan at the Rotman School.

The ideas behind *Fixing the Game* have been percolating for some time and have been helped along immensely by the encouragement of folks in the press and other thinking partners. The central idea of the book first saw the light of day in a 2003 *Barron's* editorial called "The Wrong Incentive: Executives Taking Stock Will Behave Like Athletes Placing Bets." *Barron's* editor Tom Donlon heard me talk about these ideas at a conference and invited me to write a piece for the magazine, which he edited and published.

My thinking on this front went underground for a while but resurfaced in the form of a January 2010 *Harvard Business Review* article, "The Age of Customer Capitalism," which contained a précis of the overarching argument of this book. Thanks to editor-in-chief Adi Ignatius for publishing the article in the magazine's Big Idea slot and to David Champion and Susan Donovan, the HBR editors who helped bash the article into shape. I got lots of help thinking about that article from my friends A. G. Lafley and Craig Wynett at Procter & Gamble.

The HBR article and the reactions to it got my juices flowing, and David Champion, who edits my blog series at hbr.org, encouraged and helped me to write a series of follow-up blogs on the subject. Then in the summer, Chrystia Freeland (now at Thomson Reuters), Ravi Mattu, and Stefan Stern of the *Financial Times* asked me for and helped me edit a piece for their paper called "Reward Real Growth, Not Expectations," which I really liked and which pushed my thinking further.

As my thoughts on the book progressed, I realized that there were strong links to some of my earlier work. The core of chapter 6 stems from an article that I wrote in 2002 for *Harvard Business Review* entitled "The Virtue Matrix: Calculating the Return on Corporate Responsibility." Tom Stewart (then editor-in-chief) published and Harris

Collingwood (then senior editor) assisted on that one. Chapter 5 contains thinking that flows from a 2003 *Harvard Business Review* article that I cowrote with my long-time thinking partner and coauthor Mihnea Moldoveanu entitled "Capital vs. Talent: The Battle That's Reshaping Business." Tom Stewart published the article and senior editor Anand Raman ably brought it into its final form.

Without that brainy and creative group of magazine and newspaper editors, the ideas in the book wouldn't have taken their current shape, nor would I have had the benefit of all the terrific feedback I received from readers of the various pieces. So my sincere thanks go out to all of them.

There have also been prominent investors who have encouraged me in this work. John Bogle, the founder of mutual fund giant Vanguard and author of numerous books on investing, writes me encouraging notes and quotes me in his books. Tony Arrell, founder of Burgundy Asset Management, one of Canada's leading investment management companies, and his colleague Anne Mette de Place provided encouragement and even asked me to present at the firm's annual client day. I am not an investment expert, so it was nice to receive confirmation from leaders in the field that I wasn't way off the mark!

I always send out my manuscripts to numerous friends, colleagues, and associates, and I am deeply indebted to them for their comments, corrections, watch-outs, and ideas. Thank you to Lesya Baylch-Cooper (two reviews!), Sandra Blevins, Steven Brant, David Champion, Elizabeth Edelsheim (also two reviews), Jim Fisher, Jim Hackett, Alison Kemper, Rod Lohin, Pat Meredith, Jim Milway, Robert Morris, David Naylor, Rob Pew, Joseph Rotman, David Smith, and Suzanne Spragge.

I get absolutely essential moral and managerial support from colleagues and supporters at the Rotman School. I simply couldn't write these books without taking the summers off to put fingers to the keyboard for long stretches of time. Vice deans Jim Fisher and Peter Pauly, COO Mary-Ellen Yeomans, chief of staff Suzanne Spragge, and executive assistant Kathryn Davis run the School while I am gone—and run it so well that I don't feel so guilty that I can't write. Steve Arenburg, our events guru, ran events around the world that enabled me to test out the ideas in the book with knowledgeable audiences. Ken McGuffin, our head of media relations, helped place the articles mentioned above (and numerous others). Karen Christensen, editor and publisher of *Rotman Magazine,* chipped in her sage editorial advice on my various articles.

A wonderful businessman and philanthropist named Michael Lee-Chin provided the funding to create our Institute for Corporate Citizenship, supporting the work that inspired chapter 6. Michael, thank you so very much for your foresight and generosity.

Two wonderful long-term supporters of my work at the Rotman School are Joseph Rotman, naming benefactor of the School, and Marcel Desautels, naming benefactor of the Desautels Centre for Integrative Thinking. The financial generosity of both men has made possible much of the work that I have been able to do at the Rotman School. But perhaps even more important has been their steadfast support for my writing work. Most business school deans stop writing entirely during their time in this position. Joe and Marcel have always encouraged me to follow my writing passion, and that support has been instrumental to the generation of this book. Thank you, Joe and Marcel.

This is the third book that I have had the pleasure of writing in partnership with Harvard Business Review Press senior editor Jeff Kehoe. Jeff was the catalyst who helped me shape the proposal, championed this book internally to his colleagues, provided detailed and helpful editorial advice, and nursed the project through the entire process. He is a pleasure to work with, and it feels good to have a multibook partner in Jeff and Harvard Business Review Press.

And speaking of multibook partners, a huge hug goes to my incomparable agent Tina Bennett of Janklow & Nesbit. She has been with me for each of my four sole-authored books and has been everything one could ever hope for in an agent. She shapes my proposals, places each project at the right publisher, and manages through the treacherous and changing waters of publishing contracts. I couldn't do it without you, Tina. Thanks much!

Last but not least is my partner Sandra Blevins. She has listened to me speechify on this subject more times than I care to count, read and edited numerous iterations of the manuscript, and provided valuable support throughout. Moreover, she was willing to accompany me to a remote northern cottage for my writing sabbatical in the summer of 2010, where she battled through tenacious spiders, a wandering bear, and power outages to provide companionship and loving support to me. Thanks and big hugs for everything you do, Sandra.

My closing thought is that this book represents a departure from my previous three books (*The Responsibility Virus*, *The Opposable Mind*, and *The Design of Business*) in that they were largely devoid of criticism. In this book, I am critical of some institutions (for example, hedge funds). However, I want to be clear that I bear no ill will to the people inside them. I criticize not the people but the rules of the game that have been designed, largely inadvertently, to give these institutions—and by extension the people in them—roles that fall short of helping the broader economy. My ardent belief is that if we take steps that result in fixing the game, the people in those institutions will be able to contribute more to society and experience the greater fulfillment and enjoyment of a game well-played.

ABOUT THE AUTHOR

A best-selling author, ROGER L. MARTIN is Dean of and Director of the Lee-Chin Family Institute for Corporate Citizenship at the Rotman School of Management, University of Toronto, as well as a senior adviser to CEOs of large global companies. He is a frequent contributor to *Harvard Business Review*, the *Financial Times*, *BusinessWeek*, and the *Washington Post*. In 2007, *BusinessWeek* named him one of the ten most influential business professors in the world, and in 2009, *The Times* (London) placed him thirty-second on its list of the top fifty management thinkers in the world.